> Once you choose Hope, anything's possible
>
> — Christopher Reeves

Language: English

These materials are designed to assist you in learning about hope. They should not be used for medical advice, counseling, or other health-related services. iFred, The Shine Hope Company and Kathryn Goetzke do not endorse or provide any medical advice, diagnosis, or treatment. The information provided herein should not be used for the diagnosis or treatment of any medical condition and cannot be substituted for the advice of physicians, licensed professionals, or therapists who are familiar with your specific situation. Consult a licensed medical professional, or call 911, if you are in need of immediate assistance.

ISBN: 978-1-7359395-4-4

© 2020, Kathryn Goetzke.

All rights reserved. No part of this book may be reproduced, shared or distributed without the written permission of the publisher.

For more information, please contact kathryngoetzke@theshinehopecompany.com.

Hopeful Minds is a curriculum developed by Kathryn Goetzke, Founder of the International Foundation for Research and Education on Hope (iFred) and CEO of The Shine Hope Company. It is based on research that suggests hope is a measurable and teachable skill. It impacts all outcomes in life, including academic and athletic performance, health, and resilience.

The aim is to equip children, educators, and parents with the tools they need to create, maintain, and grow hope even during the most trying times. Hope impacts an individual's ability to address economic challenges, environmental issues, job security, family relationships, and food security, so it is imperative not to underestimate the power of hope.

The focus is on prevention through practical tools and exercises. We offer all of our curriculums for download to ensure all have access, and can also be purchased online. Our program includes many activities and examples to enhance the lessons. Additionally, the program is easily adaptable to different cultures through story modifications.

The program uses a sunflower as the symbol of hope throughout. The sunflower is based on the rebranding work by iFred, using universal symbolism to create a 'brand' for hope. Consider planting sunflower gardens or fields for hope, creating sunflower artwork, or sharing the message and website so it is easier for people to find their way to our program.

We are now working to activate cities through Hopeful Cities. Find out about that program, and sign-up for our latest news, at www.theshinehopecompany.com/hopebeat-weekly

We would like to thank the following people for their contribution to our programs:

This program would not be possible without the brilliant leadership, support, and commitment to hope by:
Myron L. Belfer MD, MPA, Harvard Catalyst
Myron is Professor of Psychiatry in the Department of Psychiatry, Children's Hospital Boston, Harvard Medical School, and Senior Associate in Psychiatry at the Children's Hospital of Boston. Dr. Belfer is a Champion for Hope.

Kathryn Goetzke MBA, Author, Creator
Contributors: Taylor Steed, Katharine Lee-Kramer, Veronica O'Brien Sarah Mellen, Mic Fariscal, Anna Termulo Montances and **Naneth Samoya-Jumawid**

To our advisors, hope contributors, and experts:
Dr. Edward Barksdale, Dr. Frank Gard Jameson, Mayor Hillary Schieve, Kristy L. Stark M.A., Ed.M., BCBA, Karen Kirby PhD, MSc, BSc, C.Psychol, AfBPS, SFHEA, Ulster University, **Marie Dunne and the Northern Ireland** team that helped plant the seeds for this work.

Pioneers in early Hope Science including **Dr. Crystal Bryce, Dr. Dan Tomasulo, Dr. Chan Hellman, Dr. Matthew Gallagher, Dr. Jennifer Cheavens** and the late **Dr. Shane Lopez.**

iFred Board of Directors:
Tom Dean, Susan Minamyer, Jim Link, Dr. John Grohol, Kathryn Goetzke, Dr. Mindy Magrane

The Hopeful Minds Advisory Board

Some of our early funders: Sutter Health, Anthem, The Gordon Family Giving Fund of the Parasol Tahoe Community Foundation, The Shine Hope Company, and The Mood Factory.

IN SPECIAL RECOGNITION
Susan Minamyer, whose unconditional love, support, encouragement, faith, and brilliance planted and watered the seeds necessary to create and grow this program. Kathryn's big brothers **Arnold and Fred, and Clara, Maura, Jack, Sophie, Charles, and Sarah,** who continue to strengthen, build, and inspire Kathryn's hope.

IN HONOR
In recognition of all in the world that struggled with hopelessness in some way, shape or form, and left us way too early, including a few close to our hearts. Thank you for teaching us so much about life, love, and hope. May we spread Hope far and wide in your name and honor:
Jon and Sally Goetzke, Tom Foorman, Dr. Stephen C. Gleason, Vicky Harrison, Eloise Land, Jesse Lewis, and Austin Weirich.

TABLE OF CONTENTS

Introduction to Hopeful Minds	1
Lesson One: What and Why of Hope	8
What is Hope?	9
The Hope Matrix	10
Why is Hope Important?	11
Five Keys to Shine Hope	12
Brain and Biology	12
Allostatic Load	14
Stress Response	15
Calming Your Brain with Stress Skills	15
Happiness and Hope	16
Lesson One Overview	17
Lesson One Visuals	31
Lesson Two: Emotions and Inspired Actions	**38**
Identifying Emotions	39
Inspired Actions	39
Overcoming Obstacles	41
Lesson Two Overview	43
Lesson Two Visuals	52
Lesson Three: Challenges to Hope	**57**
The Importance of Social Connection	58
Your Hope Network	58
Challenges to Hope	60
Continuing Your Hope Journey	63
Lesson Three Overview	66
Lesson Three Visuals	77
Additional Activity: Planting Sunflowers, Growing Hope	**87**
Background Information for Educators	88
Planting Sunflowers to Learn How to Shine Hope	89
Activity Overview	91
Hopeful Minds Garden Sign	95
Sunflower Fascinating Facts Visual	96
Hopeful Minds Overview Hopework Book	**99**
Additional Resources for Educators	**132**
Curriculum Resources	133
Resources for Stress, Anxiety, and Depression	138
Where to Find Support	148

"
Let your hopes, not your hurts, shape your future.

–Robert H. Schuller

INTRODUCTION TO HOPEFUL MINDS

WELCOME TO HOPEFUL MINDS

Thank you for choosing hope. Hope is a skill every child needs to learn, as it impacts all areas of their life. By choosing this curriculum, you are taking the first step towards teaching your students critical skills that will have lasting, positive impacts on their futures.

Hopelessness is impacting our youth globally; one in seven 10-19 year olds will experience a mental health disorder, and depression, anxiety, and behavioral disorders are the leading cause of illness and disability among adolescents.

Hopelessness is the single persistent predictor of suicide. Hopelessness is also the only consistent predictor of violent behaviors in adolescents, and the only predictor of gun violence is a history of violence (APA, 2013; Demetropolous, 2017).

Additionally, hopelessness is linked to cigarette and alcohol use in college students (Jalilian et al., 2014); overdose history is also related to higher levels of hopelessness (Burns et al., 2004). Other risky behaviors associated with hopelessness in youth are unprotected sex, bullying, accidental injury, and non-suicidal self-injury (Duke et al., 2011; Larkin et al., 2013).

Hopelessness profoundly influences health outcomes, productivity, educational achievements, and human connections. Hopelessness is the primary symptom of anxiety and depression. Despite its pervasive impact, we are not taught how to recognize and actively manage hopelessness. We must strategize; suicide is the 4th leading cause of death among 15-29-year-olds globally.

We know that hopelessness is often a consequence of oppression and discrimination, so it's learned. We are teaching our kids to be hopeless, and that continues the ongoing cycle of oppression. If we want to stop the cycle of violence, self-harm, addiction, and bullying, we must start ensuring all know what hopelessness is and have the skills to activate its antidote: **HOPE**.

Higher hope is associated with higher grades, improved attention in class, reduced likelihood of anxiety and depression, less violence, less likelihood of weapon carrying in school, less likelihood of risky behaviors and addiction, better sports performance, less loneliness, and better quality relationships. Studies have found that anxiety and depression can begin to appear by age 7 and will continue to develop through middle school and high school. You can see the latest science and research on hope at Hopeful Minds: theshinehopecompany.com/research/

This introduction to Hopeful Minds is intended to give children an overview of the core components of hope. It was developed using hope theory informed by researchers around the world. This specific lesson plan is designed to give young children a broad understanding of hope, so they may understand the power of hope in their lives and learn how to create, maintain, and grow hope.

THE HOPEFUL MINDS HOPE OVERVIEW AIMS TO

- Give children a broad understanding of what hope is, why it is important, and how hope impacts all areas of their lives.
- Teach children key tools for hope, including how to generate positive feelings and take smart, inspired actions.
- Demonstrate the challenges there are to hope and how they can combat them.
- Have children create a Hope Network, and teach them that no matter what they face, there is always a way to hope.
- Encourage kids to 'aspire' to hope.

This program was designed to be used globally, as hope is a universal need. The Hopeful Minds curriculum reinforces all eight National Health Education Standards as set forth by the Centers for Disease Control and Prevention (CDC). Hopeful Mind's advancement of the National Health Education Standards is detailed at the end of this booklet.

We suggest starting with these three lessons as an overview of hope. If you are inspired, you can then complete our full curriculum, a total of 16 lessons that go more deeply into the concepts. These have been used throughout the world and across cultures, they apply to everyone and use a 'whole school approach'. Every child must learn these skills.

We recommend using this booklet with 2nd grade children, and our full, 16 lesson Hopeful Minds Deep Dive Curriculum with 5th grade children. However, most lessons can be easily adapted to fit your age group and your specific needs. We plan to also continue to add grade-specific curriculums, so please sign up for our newsletter to be alerted when new lessons become available at activate@theshinehopecompany.com.

As you continue through this curriculum, you will see that every lesson includes:

- Background information for educators about relevant research and additional resources
- Additional instructions, alternatives, and suggestions, as noted in bolded letters
- Print-outs for educators, which includes classroom displays and teacher props. All print-outs for educators are included at the end of each individual lesson.
- Lesson-specific hashtags to help you easily share the message of hope, share images that inspire you, and spread the power of hope far and wide. If you have approval, please share images of worksheets so that we can share with others, using the hashtags at the top of each lesson, tagging us @ifredorg @theshinehopecompany.
- "My Hopework Book," which includes all student worksheets and handouts. The workbook can be found on Page 91 of this booklet, or downloaded independently at www.hopefulminds.org/curriculums. You may also purchase them on Amazon or order them on IngramSparks for your bookstore if you would like printed copies.

Each lesson is intended to be 45 minutes in length. However, each lesson can be naturally split after the first activity if you choose to extend the curriculum into six lessons to allow for more discussion and activity time.

If you are not able to print the materials, the students may also write and draw on blank sheets of paper. We encourage creativity, flexibility, and adaptability; the most important thing is that we teach the "how-to" of hope. Hope must not be limited by access to resources we must innovate when it comes to hope for all.

The Hopeful Minds curriculums are continuously expanding and improving thanks to the ideas and feedback we receive from people like you. We want to make hope a viral movement around the world and we need your help. Let us know what we can do to improve the curriculums and continue making hope cool for students and educators alike by emailing us at activate@theshinehopecompany.com.

Please remember, these materials are designed to assist you in learning more about hope. They should not be used for medical advice, counseling, or other health-related services. iFred and Hopeful Minds do not endorse or provide any medical advice, diagnosis, or treatment, and are not able to field medical questions. For any such questions, please consult a licensed medical professional, or call 911 (or the appropriate emergency number in your country) if you are in need of immediate assistance.

If you have any questions at all about the program, don't hesitate to contact us at activate@theshinehopecompany.com.

HOPE SCALE

What you cannot measure, you cannot improve. It is therefore important to measure your hope levels to monitor your progress and check in on yourself. While there are many scales for hope, we use the Children and Adult Snyder Hope Scales to measure hope, as they have been used in many studies on hope. By taking the Snyder Hope Scale regularly, you can begin to see the link between hope and outcomes in every area of your life.

Hope is a journey; as you move foward, your hope levels will rise and fall. That is okay. If you practice your hope skills regularly, no matter how hopeless life seems in the low moments, you will always have a way back to hope.

We ask that you measure your hope, and encourage all those in your community to measure hope, so we can start tracking hopefulness in individuals around the world. As you work through the Hopeful Minds curriculum, have students complete the hope scale prior to starting the curriculum; then, consider administering the hope scale multiple times so the students can keep track of their hope level changes.

Use the link provided to take the Snyder Hope Scale Assessment:

www.theshinehopecompany.com/measure-your-hope/

Children's Hope Scale

Adult Hope Scale

STRENGTHS FINDER

Understanding strengths is another important tool for creating and maintaining hope. Focusing on strengths can help manage the stress response, cultivate positive thoughts, and focus on the future. Additionally, understanding strengths allows one to capitalize on their strengths while moving toward inspired actions, a necessary element in hope. Use this tool with yourself, and others. We want to focus on the children's strengths as opposed to what they are doing wrong because recognizing strengths in children can help them build confidence and support their life-long pursuit of hope. It is a positive way to create a more hopeful future.

As you work through the Hopeful Minds curriculum, have students complete the strengths assessment prior to starting the curriculum as knowing their strengths can help them while they navigate the curriculum content. You can check out your strengths, and use them with your students, here: **theshinehopecompany.pro.viasurvey.org**

HOPEFUL MINDS DEFINITION LIST

The most important terms we use in our hope curriculum, and that we hope you will start using, include:

HOPE: We define hope as a vision for something in the future, fueled by both positive feelings and inspired actions.

HOPELESSNESS: Hopelessness is both a feeling of despair and a sense of helplessness. It is emotional (a negative feeling) and motivational (an inability to act). We all experience moments of hopelessness and manage them with hope skills.

POSITIVE FEELINGS: Positive feelings are those feelings that help us to stay hopeful as we work towards our goals.

INSPIRED ACTIONS: Inspired actions are the deliberate steps you take to get in your upstairs brains and toward your goals in life.

UPSTAIRS BRAIN: This is where our thinking, imagining, problem-solving, and learning occur. This part of the brain is responsible for the development of sound decision-making and planning, control over emotions and body, and self-understanding and empathy. The upstairs brain is also where we access our positive feelings.

DOWNSTAIRS BRAIN: Also referred to as the reptilian brain, this part of the brain is responsible for basic functions such as breathing, blinking, heart rate, and fight, flight, freeze, or fawn mode. It is also responsible for the chemical stimulus associated with strong emotions, such as anger, sadness, and fear.

STRESS RESPONSE: Your stress response is when an external or internal trigger causes your brain to release stress hormones, such as cortisol, adrenaline, and norepinephrine, that force you into your fight, flight, freeze, or fawn mode. It generally lasts 90 seconds from time of the last trigger.

STRESS SKILLS: These are actions that help you navigate your stress response and work through your body's chemical response to external stimuli, to get manage your downstairs brain and get you back upstairs.

HAPPINESS HABITS: These are healthy, long-term habits that help you stay in your upstairs brain, where you access the problem-solving skills, collaboration, and passion, all critical for hope. When you take time for Happiness Habits, your brain releases happiness hormones, such as endorphins, dopamine, serotonin, and oxytocin.

NOURISHING NETWORKS: Your Nourishing Networks are the Hope Networks of the people in your life that provide you with support, help you stay on track, encourage you to succeed, and who you do the same for in return.

ELIMINATING CHALLENGES: Challenges to Hope are negative thinking patterns, like limiting beliefs, automatic negative thoughts, all-or-nothing thinking, negative bias, rumination, worry, focusing on uncontrollables, attaching to outcomes, and internalizing failure, that can keep us in hopelessness states. Eliminating challenges are the conscious act of using hope skills to overcome these challenges and get back to hope.

THE HOPE MATRIX: The Hope Matrix is the process that we use to get from hopelessness to hope. The Hope Matrix teaches us that to cultivate hope, we must move from despair to positive feelings, and from helplessness to inspired actions.

Shine Hope™: This is the mnemonic we use to remember our hope skills. Shine stands for: **S**tress Skills, **H**appiness Habits, **I**nspired Actions, **N**ourishing Networks, and **E**liminating Challenges and is what we use to activate skills for hope.

LESSON ONE

What and Why of Hope

"The one thing that we've all been needing is finally here: Hope."

-John Krasinski, Episode 8, Some Good News

LESSON ONE
WHAT AND WHY OF HOPE

WHAT IS HOPE?

How do you define hope? Have you ever really thought about it? As you read through this lesson, allow your mind to begin to mull over the idea of "hope." What does it mean when we say that you "have hope?"

Most people think of hope as a wish; a feeling of longing we have for an object or idea. However, that's not what hope is. That is not how science measures hope or how we will practice it. Hope takes the wish idea and adds thought and action to make it a reality.

There are many definitions for hope, so we will discuss a few:

- Dr. Shane Lopez, a hope expert: *"Hope is the feeling you have when you have a goal, are excited about achieving that goal, and then you figure out how you can achieve your goal."*
- Dr. Dan Tomasulo, author of *Learned Hopefulness*: *"Hope is a reorganization of perceptions to foster the belief that you have control in the future."*
- Dr. Crystal Bryce, Associate Dean of Student Affairs at University of Texas at Tyler - School of Medicine: *"Hope to me isn't squishy. Hope is something that we have control over. It is something cognitive. It's a skill. It's something that we can work toward."*
- Dr. Chan Hellman, Founding Director of the Hope Research Center: *"Hope is the belief that the future will be better than today."*

Our Founder started from the definition of hopelessness, and worked her way towards hope. As that is what she ultimately wanted to figure out - how do we get from hopelessness to hope. So she created 'The Hope Matrix' and we use this definition for hope:

HOPE is a vision for something in your future, fueled by both **POSITIVE FEELINGS** and **INSPIRED ACTIONS.**

HOPEFUL MINDS LESSON ONE: The What and Why of Hope

We created a simple image called The Hope Matrix to help you easily understand this construct. That way, no matter what challenge a person faces, you can look at The Hope Matrix and ask 'How can they best manage the Despair around this and get back to Positive Feelings' and 'How can they move from Helplessness to Inspired actions'.

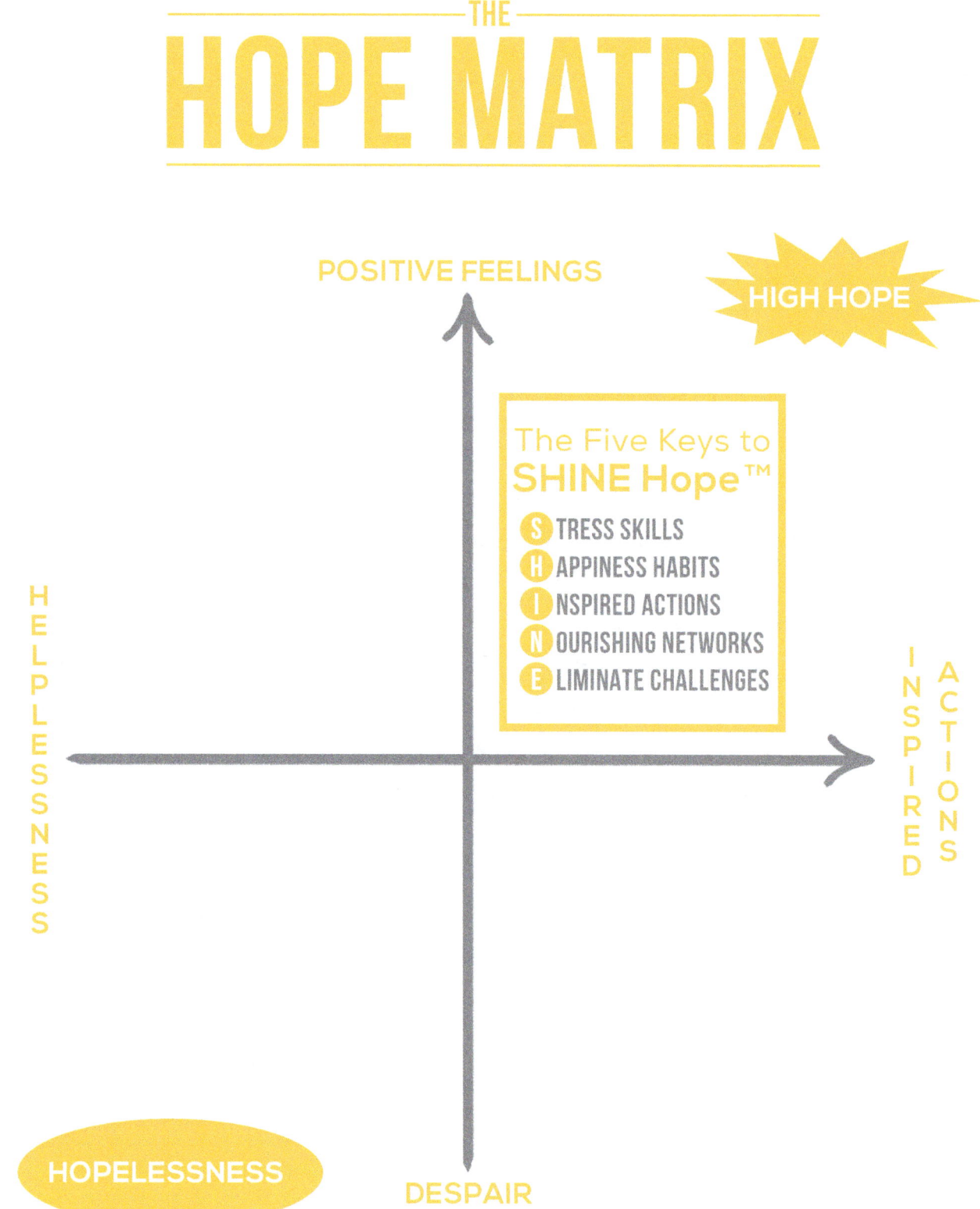

If you have hope, you must have both feelings and actions. Positive feelings are those feelings that help us to stay hopeful as we work towards our goals. Inspired actions are the steps that propel us towards our goals. It is the cycle of positive feelings and inspired actions that create and sustain hope.

WHY IS HOPE IMPORTANT?

Simply put, hope influences everything you do. Hope positively influences your academic achievements, athletic accomplishments, relationships, health, and more. It also helps you to build resiliency against anxiety, depression, hopelessness, and suicidal ideation.

Hope is a necessity in life, as it is the essence of how we overcome obstacles and resiliently grow strength from hardship. The language of hope is one that defines hardship not as an insurmountable obstacle, but as the possibility for improvement.

Well-being, success, and happiness are the side effects of hope. With hope, our futures become brighter and open to possibility. As you continue through these lessons, you will see the many ways that hope, and hope skills, can help to transform your life.

The antithesis of hope is hopelessness. Hopelessness is defined as emotional despair and motivational helplessness. It is associated with many negative life outcomes, including addictions, risky behaviors, carrying weapons at school, violence, bullying, anxiety, depression, and suicide.

HOPELESSNESS is characterized by
EMOTIONAL DESPAIR *(sadness, anger, fear)* and
MOTIVATIONAL HELPLESSNESS *(a sense of powerlessness)*

Hope is a known protective factor against hopelessness. By increasing hope, we decrease the likelihood of future hopelessness, depression, anxiety, violence, addiction, and more. By teaching these hope skills now, we can help ensure that they are integrated into your students' life practices. Our goal for this program is to help children learn hope skills early on in life to set them up for success and fulfillment both now and in the future.

HOPEFUL MINDS LESSON ONE: The What and Why of Hope

THE FIVE KEYS TO SHINE HOPE

Hope skills will be introduced during this course using the Five Keys to **Shine Hope™**. You can remember the Five Keys for Hope by remembering to always Shine Hope:

STRESS SKILLS	**H**APPINESS HABITS	**I**NSPIRED ACTIONS	**N**OURISHING NETWORKS	**E**LIMINATING CHALLENGES
90 second pause	Activating purpose	WOOP process	5:1 Rule	Limiting beliefs
Belly breathing	Pursuing passion	SMART goals	Compassion	Automatic Negative Thoughts (ANTs)
Journaling	Utilizing strengths	Stretch goals	Forgiveness	All-or-nothing thinking
Gardening	Meditation	Achievement goals	Love	Negative bias
Calming music	Smiling	Intrinsic goals	Gratitude	Rumination & Worry
Affirming beliefs	Exercising / Nutrition	Mastery goals	Recognition	Focusing on uncontrollables
Sensory engagement	Creating / listening to music	Micro goals / Stepping	Support	Attaching to outcomes
Cold plunge	Dancing / Singing	Habit stacking	Faith	Internalizing failure
Decluttering	Drawing / Painting	Visualization	Trust	Toxic consumption
Prayer	Gratitude	Overcoming obstacles	Respect	Nocebo effect
Nature walk	Volunteering	Regoaling	Effective listening	Mind wandering
Napping	Wonder/Awe	Write down goals / check in	Empathy	Implicity bias
Laughter	Quality sleep		Kindness	Negative framing
Crying	Doodling		Animals	Perfectionism
Tapping				Taking things personally
Yoga				
Mantras				

The acronym "Shine" introduces each of these Five Keys to Shine Hope, making it easy to remember how to create, maintain, and cultivate hope in life.

BRAIN AND BIOLOGY

It's important to understand the connection between your brain, body, and behavior so you can begin to use it to your advantage. When your mood changes, it may be so subtle that you don't pick up on it at first. However, your body does, and it reacts. These are known as psychosomatic responses. For example, when I am triggered, I grind my teeth, my shoulders clench, and I sometimes even forget to breathe. All of these reactions are caused by the relationship between my brain and biology.

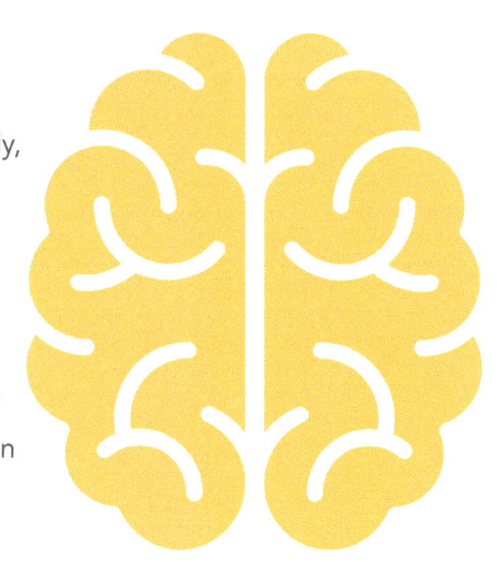

The relationship between your body and brain is woven by complex circuitry, meaning that they influence one another in various ways that can be hard to identify in our own lives. Psychosomatic responses are manifestations of the state of your brain in your physical body, they can come in the form of discomfort, sensations, or habits. Behavior under stress is often the culmination of thoughts and feelings, and while this can sometimes seem problematic, like when you snap at someone because you are stressed, it can also be incredibly beneficial. When you look at the connection between your brain, biology, and behavior through the lens of hope, you can start to reframe how you think and feel.

Increasing hope isn't just about influencing your brain; it is also about positively impacting your biology and behavior. When you positively impact your brain, you are also providing long-term benefits.

THE DOWNSTAIRS BRAIN, The downstairs brain includes the limbic system, brainstem, and amygdala. It is the more primitive part of the brain (also referred to as the reptilian brain), and is responsible for basic functions such as breathing, blinking, heart rate, and fight, flight, or freeze mode. The downstairs brain is also responsible for the chemical stimulus associated with strong emotions, such as anger, rage, sadness, frustration, and fear.

THE UPSTAIRS BRAIN, Your upstairs brain is also known as the prefrontal cortex. It is where your thinking, imagining, learning, problem-solving, and creativity all occur. This part of your brain is responsible for the development of sound decision-making and planning, self-understanding, and empathy. The upstairs brain is also where you feel positive emotions, such as happiness, contentment, peace, and passion. You may remember that positive feelings are the first ingredient of hope; this means that you can only access your hope when you are in your upstairs brain.

It's important to remember that the downstairs brain is not a "bad" part of your brain. It is important for survival and it helps us understand the world around us. However, you don't want to be in your downstairs brain all the time. The hope skills you are going to learn during this program will help you move from your downstairs brain into your upstairs brain so that you can always return to a hopeful mindset.

ALLOSTATIC LOAD

We all experience stress, it's entirely normal. Experts[1] believe we need a certain amount of stress to function at an optimum level because stress motivates us to make changes and reach our goals.

However, persistent stress leads to many negative consequences that can have a lasting effect on our overall health and well-being; this is called the allostatic load. We experience the allostatic load when the challenges we face in our environment exceed our ability to cope.

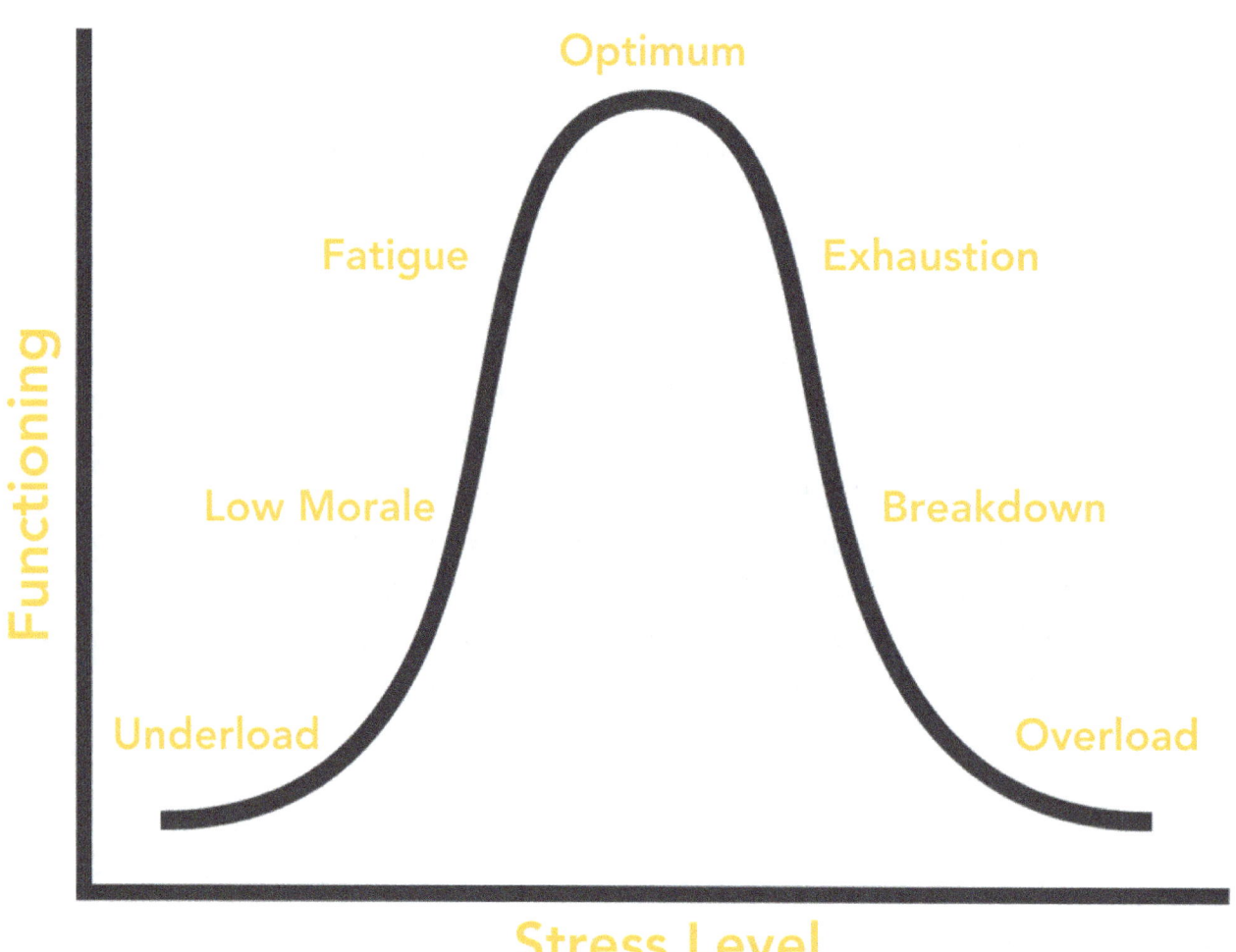

[1] news.berkeley.edu/2013/04/16/researchers-find-out-why-some-stress-is-good-for-you/

THE STRESS RESPONSE

Dr. Jill Bolte Taylor came up with the 90-second rule in her book, "My Stroke of Insight" to explain the biology behind your stress response. The 90-second rule says that when you are triggered by something in your environment, a chemical process takes place in your body for approximately 90 seconds. For 90 seconds after the environmental trigger, your body is flooded with stress hormones, such as adrenaline, cortisol, and norepinephrine, that force you into your fight, flight, freeze, or fawn mode (aka your downstairs brain).

Identifying a stress response when it occurs and finding a hopeful way out of it is crucial to return to a stable state of mind and body. While we don't want to ignore our emotions, what we want to do is get a handle on what they are trying to tell us, and let them help us move forward. In order to do that, we also have to proactively manage the physiological response to stress.

CALMING YOUR BRAIN WITH STRESS SKILLS

The First Key to Shine Hope is related to the **"S"** in Shine: **Stress Skills**. Stress Skills are skills that help you navigate your 90-second physiological response, manage your stress response, and re-enter your upstairs brain. Your Stress Skills should cater to how you feel during stress. For example, if stress makes you avoidant, you should try a behavior-changing Stress Skill like going for a walk or reaching out to a friend. If you experience psychosomatic responses like freezing or anger, you could try a Stress Skill that activates your body and your happiness. Finding Stress Skills that combat your downstairs brain are key, so identifying the negative habits or psychosomatic responses which occur for you during stress will help you to select Stress Skills. Most of all, Stress Skills are designed to be tried, so don't be afraid to try several until you find the ones that work for you.

Stress Skills include short activities such as:

- 90 Second Pause
- Deep Belly Breathing
- Napping
- Calming Music
- Reaffirming beliefs
- Visualization
- Sensory Engagement
- Punching a Pillow
- Crying
- Prayer
- Walk in Nature
- Meditation
- Yoga
- Decluttering
- Focus on Strengths
- Journaling
- Exercise
- Gardening
- Time Near Water and Nature

While these are some of our favorite Stress Skills, they are not the only ones. It's important that you find Stress Skills that work for you when you are triggered. What works for your friend or roommate won't necessarily work for you. You may need to try several Stress Skills before you find one that works for you.

HAPPINESS AND HOPE

The Second Key to Shine Hope is related to the **"H"** in Shine: **Happiness Habits.** Happiness Habits are healthy, long-term actions that you can take to foster positive feelings and stay in your upstairs brain.

Happiness makes hope visible to us. When we are happy or reminded of happiness, our sense of hope becomes more possible. The longest study of adult life ever carried out followed two groups of individuals from different backgrounds throughout their lives and investigated how and why these people were able to thrive throughout adulthood. The result was quite simple: researchers found that taking care of ourselves physically and being a part of healthy relationships leads to a longer and happier life.

When you perform your Happiness Habits, your brain releases endorphins, dopamine, serotonin, and oxytocin, the four horsemen of happiness. When these chemicals are released, you experience increased levels of happiness, which in turn fosters positive feelings. When you maintain daily Happiness Habits, you are ensuring future happiness and hope.

Some of our favorite Happiness Habits include:

- Utilizing strengths
- Pursuing passion
- Activating purpose
- Smiling
- Exercising
- Playing or Listening to Music
- Spending time in Nature
- Showing Gratitude and Kindness
- Playing Games
- Volunteering
- Time with Family and Friends
- Experiencing Wonder & Awe
- Practicing Faith
- Sleeping
- Nutrition
- Dancing and Singing
- Donating
- Giving a hug
- Setting Goals
- Practicing Affirmations

Many of us already have Happiness Habits in the hobbies we do, the things we do in our free time that make us happy. Happiness Habits are incredibly important for your physical and mental health. When you practice healthy, long-term Happiness Habits, they create numerous positive outcomes, including improved self-confidence, good sleep, better memory retention, relief of anxiety and depression, improved health, and energy towards goal achievement.

 Additional Resources for Educators

- Explaining the Brain to Children and Adolescents
- Heart Rate Variability: A New Way to Track Well-Being
- Gain Hope: A Place for Hope in the Age of Anxiety
- Fight, Flight, Freeze Responses
- John Krasinski Biography
- Some Good News

Links to resources can be found on Page 116

HOPEFUL MINDS LESSON ONE: The What and Why of Hope

LESSON 1 OVERVIEW
Total Instruction Time: 45 Minutes

FORMAT
Instructor Reading and Discussion
My Hopework Book Worksheet
Instructor Reading and Discussion
My Hopework Book Worksheet
Breathing Exercise
Instructor Reading and Discussion
My Hopework Book Worksheets
Instructor Reading and Discussion

LESSON OBJECTIVES
Define Hope
Understand How Hope Affects our Brains
Identifying Stress Skills
Identifying Happiness Habits

PRINT-OUTS FOR EDUCATORS
Classroom Hope Sunflower Center
Classroom Hope Sunflower Petals
Stop. Breathe. Relax. Visual for Classroom
Five Keys to Shine Hope Visual
Stress Skills Visual
Happiness Habits Visual

PRINT-OUTS FOR STUDENTS
The Hope Matrix (optional: My Hopework book Page 7)
Five Keys to Shine Hope (My Hopework book Page 8)
STOP. BREATHE. RELAX (My Hopework book Page 9)
Happiness Habits (My Hopework book Page 10)
My Hope Sunflower (My Hopework book Page 11)

LESSON 1 OUTLINE

📖	10 Minutes	"What is Hope?" Educator Reading and Class Discussion
📄	5 Minutes	My Hopework Book: My Hope SunFlower
📖	5 Minutes	"Your Brain and Hope" Educator Reading (My Hopework Book: Shine Worksheet, My Hopework Book: STOP. BREATHE. RELAX Worksheet)
👣	10 Minutes	Activity: Belly Breathing Exercise
📄	5 Minutes	Happiness Habits (My Hopework Book: Happiness Habits)
📄	5 Minutes	My Hopework Book: My Hope SunFlower
📄	5 Minutes	Hope Hero Spotlight: John Krasinski
💬	Remaining	Final Discussion (Optional)

LESSON 1 PREPARATION

Prior to the lesson, prepare the following materials:

- Print out your Classroom Hope Sunflower and hang it somewhere where the students can see it
- Print out "Stop. Breathe. Relax" visual and hang it somewhere where the students can see it (optional)
- Print out My Hope Sunflower worksheets for students
- Print out Hope worksheets for students
- Print out happiness habits visual

WHAT IS HOPE?
10 Minutes

Read the following to the students:

Today we are going to learn about hope. Raise your hand if you think you know what hope is? *(Acknowledge students for raising their hands)*

Great! Today we're going to learn more about hope, why it is so important to you, and how we can all make our hope muscles stronger. Did you know that hope predicts how well you do in sports? Who here wants to be really good at sports? *(Acknowledge students for raising hands)*

Did you know that hope also predicts how well you will do on tests? Who here wants to get good grades? *(Acknowledge students for raising hands)*

And did you know that having higher levels of hope will also help you have better friendships? Who here wants to have good friends? *(Acknowledge students for raising hands)*

Having high hope can also make you healthy and strong. Who here wants to be healthy? *(Acknowledge students for raising hands)*

Great! As you can see, hope is incredibly important because it can make your life better.

So what is hope?

WHAT IS HOPE? CNT'D

Doctors and scientists who study hope believe that hope is the feeling you get when you have a goal, you are excited about your goal, and then you figure out how to reach your goal. For example, with hope, you can be better at sports or get better grades!

There are two important ingredients that make up hope: **positive feelings** and **inspired actions.** Let's talk about those two ingredients.

Positive feelings are feelings that bring us closer to hope. Positive feelings give us a positive charge that gives us the energy to be hopeful. Can you name some positive feelings? *(Ask for responses - Happiness, joy, gratitude, love, peace, excitement, humor, playfulness, etc.)*

Inspired actions are actions that help us be hopeful and reach our goals. Inspired actions can be anything from eating healthy to exercising to being creative.

With these two ingredients- positive feelings and inspired actions- we can start to have more hope in our lives.

You may be wondering why hope is so important. Well, the opposite of hope is hopelessness, which is defined as emotional despair and motivational helplessness. Hopeless is related to many negative events in life such as depression, bullying, anxiety, and suicide.

We know that hope protects against hopelessness, so we have to work to increase our hope. But, hope is not something you are born with. It is something you have to practice and develop. Like basketball.

What is something you have to do to become a really good basketball player? *(Ask for responses - dribbling, shooting, running, etc.)*

When you want to be good at basketball, you have to practice all of your skills so that you get stronger and faster.

If you want to be better at sports or get better grades, hope helps! How? Let's say you want to learn to dribble because it will help you be a better basketball player. If you can't dribble right away when you start to practice, you might get frustrated and give up.

WHAT IS HOPE? CNT'D

This is where hope can help! Hope helps us have positive feelings when we are working towards our goals. Instead of getting frustrated, our hope skills can help us keep a positive mindset and learn to dribble. Our inspired actions can help us learn how to dribble more quickly.

Being hopeful also makes us strong emotionally. Whenever you face something that is hard or scary, having hope can help you beat it.

The best thing about hope is that anyone can be hopeful. It doesn't matter who your parents are, who your friends are, where you live, how much money you have, what people do to you, what people say about you, or your background.

Your hope is up to you, and you have control. Absolutely anyone can learn hope and be good at it. And if you practice your hope skills, you can be hopeful no matter what. And remember, hope predicts so many great things in life.

So, let's talk about what hope means to us!

Discuss the following questions with your class:

- What does the word hope mean to you?
- How does the word hope make you feel?
- What is something that you feel hopeful for today? This week? This year?

SUNFLOWER ACTIVITY
MY HOPEWORK BOOK PAGE 11
5 Minutes

As you answer the questions above, have the class come up with a classroom definition for hope. Write this definition in the center of your classroom Hope Sunflower and then place the flower on your wall so your students can see it.

Have each student turn to My Hopework Book Page 11 (My Hope Sunflower) and write their own personal definition of hope in the center of their flower.

HOPE DEFINITION EXAMPLES:

- Hope is feeling that you want something to happen and working hard to make it happen.

- Hope is a vision, fueled by positive feelings and inspired action.

- Hope is that little feeling inside of you that keeps you moving forward.

YOUR BRAIN AND HOPE
5 Minutes

Read the following to the students:

Now that we know what hope is, and how it can help us be more successful, we are going to talk about how hope tools can also improve how our brains work.

We have two different parts of our brain: the upstairs brain and the downstairs brain. Can you visualize stairs in your brain? *(Acknowledge student responses)*

First, let's walk up the stairs to the upstairs brain. The upstairs brain controls more complicated actions, like making good decisions, understanding yourself, and being better friends, as well as positive feelings, such as happiness, excitement, and joy. We use our upstairs brain and our hope skills to learn new things. Can you see these in your upstairs brain? *(Acknowledge student responses)*

Now, let's walk down the stairs to our downstairs brain. The downstairs brain controls our survival instincts. In our downstairs brain, we feel strong emotions like anger, sadness, and fear. These feelings can be very strong. Can you feel these emotions in your downstairs brain? *(Acknowledge student responses)*

Imagine a zebra. When a zebra is attacked by a lion, it has to make a really quick decision; it can try to fight the lion, it can run away from the lion, or it can freeze and do nothing. This is called fight, flight, or freeze. The zebra only sees three options: it can fight, run away, or freeze. Fight, flight, or freeze decisions are made with the downstairs brain. Can you remember a time when you were scared? Can you see your downstairs brain at work?

YOUR BRAIN AND HOPE CNT'D

The problem is, only one portion of our brain can work at a time. That means, when the zebra is trying to make a fight, flight, or freeze decision, it can't talk to its upstairs brain to see if there is another good option. The zebra is too scared, so the downstairs brain is in control. Can you be upstairs and downstairs in a building at the same time? No!

We are the same way. When we get angry or scared, we act just like the zebra. We might not be chased by a lion, but we do have the same fight, flight, or freeze decisions. For example, if someone makes us angry, we might decide to hit them, or if someone is mean to us we might choose to run away and hide.

While these decisions might feel right in the moment, we know that in the long term they are usually the wrong decision. That's because we make these decisions with our downstairs brain. When we let our downstairs brain take over, we ignore any of the good ideas that our upstairs brain might have.

- When are some times that you use your downstairs brain?
- What did you feel when you were angry or scared?

When you get angry or scared, you might notice that your heart starts pounding really fast and it can get hard to breathe. Sometimes it can be really hard to think, and your brain might feel like it is screaming. Can anybody relate? *(Acknowledge student responses)*

This is when the biology of our body gets really activated. The more we think about fear, the more our body is reacting to fear, and the more we feel fear. Do you see how this works? *(Acknowledge student responses)*

Our biology impacts our behavior. And our behavior impacts our biology. This cycle continues and makes it grow worse. So when we feel our body getting stressed, it means we're in our downstairs brain. Have you all heard the word "getting stressed out?" This is what this means. We are constantly in fight or flight, and "stressed out."

The problem is, hope is in our upstairs brain. Hope helps us overcome our anger and fear. It helps us learn how to recognize the anger in other people and take smart steps for ourselves so we don't make the situation worse. Remember, we can't be upstairs and downstairs at the same time. So we need to get back to our upstairs brain.

Thankfully, the first of our hope skills can help us.

STRESS SKILLS

During the next few lessons, we are going to learn five important hope skills that will help us keep our hope strong. They are the Five Keys to Shine Hope and can be remembered using the mnemonic "Shine." Who knows how to spell shine? *(Acknowledge responses)*

Turn to page 8 in your Hopework book and we will fill in what each of the letters for Shine stands for together.

Each letter in Shine stands for one of our hope skills:
Stress Skills, **H**appiness Habits, **I**nspired Actions, **N**ourishing Networks, **E**liminating Challenges

When we Shine Hope, it means that we are using all of our hope skills!

Let's talk about the first Key to Shine Hope: Stress Skills. When we are stressed, Stress Skills help us calm down and go from our downstairs brain to our upstairs brain.

STRESS SKILLS INCLUDE:

- 90 Second Pause
- Deep Belly Breathing
- Napping
- Calming Music
- Reaffirming beliefs
- Visualization
- Sensory Engagement

- Punching a Pillow
- Crying
- Prayer
- Walk in Nature
- Meditation
- Yoga
- Decluttering

- Focus on Strengths
- Journaling
- Exercise
- Gardening
- Time Near Water and Nature

Have students turn to page 6 of the Hopework Book: "STOP. BREATHE. RELAX." Then have students circle their four favorite stress skills. Once completed, read the following:

When something makes you angry or scared, your downstairs brain takes over for at least 90 seconds, and our stress response kicks in. That's a long time! Because it takes over for at least 90 seconds, it's important that we practice calming down for at least 90 seconds.

STRESS SKILLS CNT'D

Anytime you are angry, overwhelmed, or stressed, taking some deep breaths can help you calm down your downstairs brain. Taking deep breaths is important because it keeps you from responding when you are in your downstairs brain. When your downstairs brain is in charge and you respond with negative emotions, you can do things that you might regret later. Next time you're upset, remember to breathe deeply; this will help you get back into your upstairs brain.

We are going to practice this, right now, together.

BELLY BREATHING EXERCISE
10 Minutes

The easiest way to teach belly breathing is to demonstrate deep breathing and then ask students to join you.

BELLY BREATHING INSTRUCTIONS:

- Sit in a comfortable position with your back as straight as possible.
- Notice how your body feels. Take a few seconds to just relax. Relax your neck, shoulders, arms, legs, and feet. Try a few big exhales.
- When you're ready, place one hand on your chest and the other on your belly button (below the rib cage).
- Now take a long, slow, deep breath in through your nose for a count of 10 (or as long as you are able). As you breathe in, you want to send the air to your belly button. Your hand on your belly should rise while the hand on your chest remains still.
- Once you get to 10, slowly exhale out of your mouth. Feel the muscles of your stomach tighten and your hand lower.

Do this for at least 90 seconds (or 10 slow, deep breaths)

BELLY BREATHING EXERCISE CNT'D

Deep breathing is most effective if done for at least 3 minutes. If you practice deep breathing with your class, try to increase by one breath each time until you reach 3 minute sessions.

Once the students have practiced their deep breathing, read the following:

- How do you feel after deep breathing? Do you feel any different?
- You can do deep breathing anywhere, anytime. Even a few deep breaths will help calm you down, especially when you're really angry (your big brother is yelling) or scared (a weird sound woke you up).
- Deep breathing is one of the most important hope tools that we can use. If you want to have really strong hope, it's important to practice deep breathing 2-3 times each day.
- You can also use deep breathing to help other people. When your friends or siblings use their downstairs brain because they are angry or scared, you can teach them how to use their deep breathing to calm down too!

Deep breathing can be a great way to help de-escalate classroom disputes.

Consider making it a classroom policy to have agitated students take several deep breaths before talking to you.

HAPPINESS HABITS
5 Minutes

Now, let's talk about the second Key to Shine Hope: Happiness Habits. When we are in our upstairs brain, we want to use skills to stay there. Happiness habits are things we can do that help us stay happy long term.

HAPPINESS HABITS INCLUDE THINGS LIKE:

- Utilizing strengths
- Pursuing passion
- Activating purpose
- Smiling
- Exercising
- Playing or Listening to Music
- Spending time in Nature
- Showing Gratitude and Kindness
- Playing Games
- Volunteering
- Time with Family and Friends
- Experiencing Wonder & Awe
- Practicing Faith
- Sleeping
- Nutrition
- Dancing and Singing
- Donating
- Giving a hug
- Setting Goals
- Practicing Affirmations

You might have noticed that eating healthy food was on that list. Healthy foods like fruits and vegetables help our brains. Not only is it healthy for our bodies, but it is also healthy for our hope! Fruits and vegetables help our moods improve, which means they also help our hope improve.

When we want to switch from bad feelings to happiness feelings, we now know how to practice our deep breathing like we learned earlier in the lesson.

All of these Happiness Habits also help us feel hope! The things you can do to increase happiness and hope are as limitless as your imagination. Now that we've reviewed Happiness Habits, pick out and circle your favorite four on your Happiness Habits worksheet (page 7).

As a class, finish filling in the class sunflower with four Happiness Habits and four Stress Skills, then have students individually complete their sunflowers (page 8) with the four Happiness Habits and Stress Skills they circled on the Happiness Habits worksheet and STOP. BREATHE. RELAX worksheet.

MY HOPE HERO
JOHN KRASINSKI
5 Minutes

Read the following story out loud to the students:

Who knows who John Krasinski is? *(Show picture to class for reference)*

John Krasinski is one of the most popular actors in Hollywood. He has been in lots of different TV shows and movies, like the Office. However, out of all of his shows and movies, his most recent show has been Some Good News. Has anyone seen his show Some Good News on YouTube? *(Acknowledge students who raise their hands)*

A few years ago, John was watching the news and realized that news channels only show sad stories, even though there are lots of great things happening in the world every day. When the coronavirus pandemic happened, the news channels got even sadder. Who agrees? *(Acknowledge students who raise their hands)*

John knew that people needed hope to help them overcome the hopelessness they were feeling. John decided he needed to do something to help people focus on the first ingredient of hope. Who remembers what the first ingredient of hope is? *(Answer: Positive feelings)*

John talks about how he cried, and while he was sad about the pandemic, he didn't want to stay sad because he couldn't change the pandemic. He could not control it. So he released his sadness, got out of the downstairs brain and into the upstairs brain, and got creative about what he could do to lift people's spirits.

John decided that, to help people focus on positive feelings, he would make a news channel that only reported good news. Every week, John started releasing a new episode of his show and people loved it!

On Some Good News, John focused on happy things happening around the world. He threw virtual parties for students who graduated and nurses and doctors who were working hard to fight coronavirus, he shared stories of recoveries, he let people video chat with their favorite celebrities, and he shared the happy videos that people sent him.

HOPE HERO SPOTLIGHT CNT'D

John used many Stress Skills, like helping others, talking to his friends, and putting on a show, to keep his hopeful mindset. He also helped other people stay hopeful by showing them that positive feelings are a key ingredient for hope.

John understands the importance of hope, and he works hard to make sure that other people understand it too. As he tells everyone in his show: "No matter how hard things get, there is always good in the world."

Just like John, it is our job to use our hope tools to keep hope in our lives and to share hope with others.*

*This story was created from publicly available information. It does not suggest endorsement of Hopeful Minds, or any affiliation by known celebrity to our program. All information is for illustrative purposes for youth, to demonstrate skills used to create, maintain, and grow hope.

FINAL DISCUSSION

Discuss the following questions with your class:

- How was hope important to John?
- Do you think hope is important in your life?
- How many of you now want to become more hopeful?
- How do you think we can make hope skills cool and fun so that everyone wants to do them to increase hope in their lives?

Let us know if you or your students come up with new ways to make hope cool by emailing us at *activate@theshinehopecompany.com*.

ADDITIONAL ACTIVITIES FOR HOME OR VIRTUAL LEARNING

Consider using the following "Hopework" activities to help students enhance their hope skills:

- Complete the "Hope Matrix" worksheet (My Hopework Book Page 7) to help visualize where hope and hopelessness fall within the spectrum of hope. Have students fill in the matrix using the words at the bottom of the page based on what they've learned during Lesson 1.
- Have students color in their Shine worksheet (My Hopework Book Page 8) and display them around the classroom.
- Journaling and drawing can be great ways to help students identify the source of the emotions they are feeling. Consider having students use the blank Hope Journal pages at the back of the My Hopework Books to journal about or draw their responses to the following prompts:
    - What can they control about the school year?
    - What can't they control?
    - How can they make the most of what they can control?
    - How can they release emotions from what they can't control?
    - How can they make distance learning more fun?
    - What can the teacher do to make it engaging and interesting?
    - How can they make it fun for others?
    - How can they be creative about their experience this semester or year?

MY HOPE SUNFLOWER

HOPE SUNFLOWER PETALS

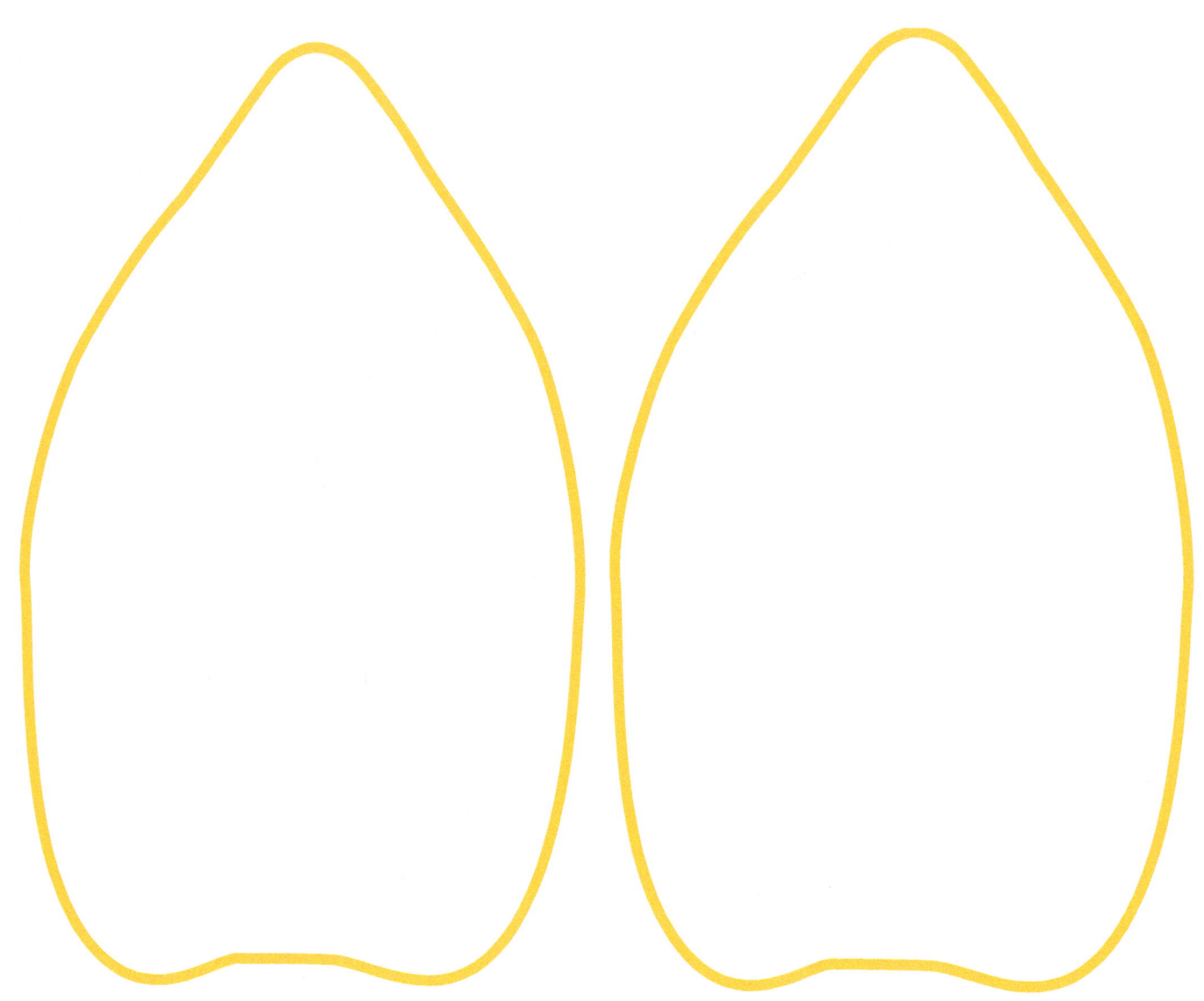

STOP. *BREATHE.* RELAX.

Directions: Circle your top four favorite stress skills from the list below. If there are additional stress skills you use that are not on the list, use the space below the add them.

Stress Skills

- 90 Second Pause
- Deep Belly Breathing
- Napping
- Calming Music
- Reaffirming beliefs
- Visualization
- Sensory Engagement
- Punching a Pillow
- Crying
- Prayer
- Walk in Nature
- Meditation
- Yoga
- Decluttering
- Focus on Strengths
- Journaling
- Exercise
- Gardening
- Time Near Water and Nature

MY FAVORITE STRESS SKILLS

-
-
-
-
-
-
-

SHINE HOPE™
A HOW-TO FOR HOPE IN TRYING TIMES

Scan the code to measure hope with the **Hope Scale!**

S TRESS SKILLS
- 90 second pause
- Belly breathing
- Journaling
- Gardening
- Calming music
- Affirming beliefs
- Sensory engagement
- Cold plunge
- Decluttering
- Prayer
- Nature walk
- Napping
- Laughter
- Crying
- Tapping
- Yoga
- Mantras

H APPINESS HABITS
- Activating purpose
- Pursuing passion
- Utilizing strengths
- Meditation
- Smiling
- Exercising / Nutrition
- Creating / listening to music
- Dancing / Singing
- Drawing / Painting
- Gratitude
- Volunteering
- Wonder/Awe
- Quality sleep
- Doodling

I NSPIRED ACTIONS
- WOOP process
- SMART goals
- Stretch goals
- Achievement goals
- Intrinsic goals
- Mastery goals
- Micro goals / Stepping
- Habit Stacking
- Visualization
- Overcoming obstacles
- Regoaling
- Write down goals / check in

N OURISHING NETWORKS
- 5:1 Rule
- Compassion
- Forgiveness
- Love
- Gratitude
- Recognition
- Support
- Faith
- Trust
- Respect
- Effective Listening
- Empathy
- Kindness
- Animals

E LIMINATING CHALLENGES
- Limiting beliefs
- Automatic Negative Thoughts (ANTs)
- All-or-nothing thinking
- Negative bias
- Rumination & Worry
- Focusing on Uncontrollables
- Attaching to outcomes
- Internalizing failure
- Toxic Consumption
- Nocebo Effect
- Mind Wandering
- Implicity Bias
- Negative Framing
- Perfectionism
- Taking things personally

© The Shine Hope Company, LLC

the shine hope company

STRESS SKILLS

Stress Skills are actions that help you navigate your stress response and work through your body's chemical response to external stimuli. By practicing them, you are teaching yourself how to proactively manage the emotional despair found in hopelessness and move towards positive feelings where you activate hope.

The Stress Response

This is when you are emotionally triggered by something in your environment, and you go into fight, flight, freeze, or fawn mode as your body releases stress hormones, such as cortisol, adrenaline, and norepinephrine. You are in your downstairs brain, and can't reach your upstairs brain; the upstairs brain is the place where you make good decisions for moving towards all you hope for in life.

90 second pause	Sensory engagement	Laughter
Belly breathing	Cold plunge	Crying
Journaling	Decluttering	Tapping
Gardening	Prayer	Yoga
Calming music	Nature walk	Mantras
Affirming beliefs	Napping	

© The Shine Hope Company, LLC

HAPPINESS HABITS

Happiness Habits are healthy, long-term actions that cause your brain to release happiness hormones including endorphins, dopamine, serotonin, and oxytocin. Happiness Habits help you stay in your upstairs brain, where you access the problem-solving skills, collaboration, and passion critical for hope.

Positive Feelings

Positive feelings, the first ingredient of hope, are feelings that are located in your upstairs brain like wonder, joy, and peace that make it easier to overcome obstacles that get in the way of hope. You proactively manage the emotional despair of hopelessness using Stress Skills and use your Happiness Habits to stay in your upstairs brain, where you then energetically move towards your goals in life.

Activating purpose	**Exercising / Nutrition**	**Volunteering**
Pursuing passion	**Creating / listening to music**	**Wonder/Awe**
Utilizing strengths	**Dancing / Singing**	**Quality sleep**
Meditation	**Drawing / Painting**	**Doodling**
Smiling	**Gratitude**	

© The Shine Hope Company, LLC

"The one thing that we've all been needing is finally here: Hope."

– John Krasinski
Episode 8, Some Good News

LESSON TWO

Emotions and Inspired Actions

"All kids need is a little help, a little hope and somebody who believes in them."

-Magic Johnson

LESSON TWO
EMOTIONS AND INSPIRED ACTIONS

IDENTIFYING EMOTIONS

Knowing Stress Skills and Happiness Habits are just the beginning. To appropriately apply these skills, we must have the ability to recognize and label emotions, and this is something a lot of people struggle with because we don't teach emotions in schools. Yet managing our emotions is key to getting all we hope for in life.

Many cultures have engrained the idea that 'negative' emotions should be suppressed and that if we are not happy, we should not express the emotion. Yet that is not true! Emotions are so important, and tell us what we care about. If used appropriately, they can be major energy for good. Negative emotions, once we learn from them, are fuel to create a better world for all of us.

Some people have also never had exposure to the language necessary to describe emotions. However, it's vital that we have the ability to identify our emotions. The primary purpose of emotional awareness is that it allows us to know what we need in life. Emotions are like our internal compass and recognizing them allows us to help navigate our downstairs brain, learn what we care about, and use skills to manage them and get back upstairs. When we embrace the negative emotions and learn from them, we don't need things like food or substances to make us feel better, as we now have internal tools and knowledge to make ourselves feel better. And that is where our power lies.

INSPIRED ACTIONS

The Third Key to Shine Hope is related to the **"I"** in Shine: **Inspired Actions.**

Once we learn to manage our emotions and get in the upstairs brain, we practice inspired actions by creating SMART (specific, measurable, attainable, relevant, time-bound) goals. SMART goals give us something to look forward to and encourage us to work toward our future, or all we hope for in life. The SMART goals we set may change over time; it is our ability to adapt and set new goals that ultimately indicate how hopeful we stay in life.

SMART goals should always be set from a place of positive feelings. When goals are set from a place of stress or anxiety, it is often the case that we don't set the goals from a place of inspiration, but instead fear. When this happens, our goals can actually move us in the opposite direction of our desires.

One of the causes of hopelessness is setting an unrealistic goal or having set our goal from a place of negativity. When we set goals that are confusing, broad, unspecific, stemming from anger or fear, or impractical, we are setting ourselves up for failure. Instead, we should be setting SMART goals that will encourage us to continue moving forward with positive feelings and inspired actions.

Keep in mind, SMART goals are just one framework, and we get more advanced in our hope programming we also talk about why some 'Stretch' goals are also important, as it helps us think about shooting for the moon. Yet SMART is a good starting framework, and something that can really help set you up for success.

SMART GOALS SHOULD BE

Specific: Be specific about your goal. Think about these questions when creating your goal: What needs to be accomplished? Who is responsible for it? What steps will you take to achieve it?

Measurable: Can you measure your progress? If this goal will take a long time to achieve, set shorter-term goals to reach along the way.

Achievable: Are you inspired and motivated to reach your goal? Do you have the tools or skills you need? If not, do you know how you can get them?

Relevant: Does your goal make sense? Does it go along with what you are trying to achieve in the bigger picture?

Time-bound: Is your timing realistic? Can you achieve your goal in the time period set? Think about what you may want to achieve at the halfway point.

"SMART"-goal-setting is an evidence-based approach that is used universally at any scale – from individual goals to big business strategies. We want to strengthen our hope through positive feelings and, in turn, this inspired and SMART action.

Commit to inspired action steps: Once you have a goal, determine the steps you will need to take to complete it. A goal is guaranteed to fail if you never take any steps to reach it. Luckily, you should have identified most of the inspired steps you will need to take using your SMART goal questions.

OVERCOMING OBSTACLES

Whenever you work towards goals, running into obstacles is inevitable. Therefore, it is important that you learn to handle obstacles in a healthy way. When you see your obstacles as a threat or look at them with feelings of despair and helplessness (the ingredients of hopelessness), you are much more likely to let them keep you from reaching your goals.

Instead, frame obstacles in a more positive way. Try to see each obstacle you encounter as an interesting puzzle to solve or an opportunity to grow. Every path will have obstacles. Therefore, if you want to be hopeful and continue moving forward, you have to learn how to face them head-on.

You can also make the obstacles you face seem much less intimidating by practicing some techniques for overcoming obstacles:

Prepare for Potential Obstacles: When you set goals, you should also think critically about the obstacles you may encounter. By visualizing your obstacles and their solutions ahead of time, you increase your ability to overcome them when they arise.

Identify Multiple Pathways: Identifying multiple ways to achieve your goal can allow you to sidestep potential obstacles you may encounter.

Ask For Help When You Need It: Asking for ideas from others can be very helpful when overcoming obstacles. Other people are likely to have skills or resources that you don't have. We will talk more about asking for help later in this course.

Break it Down: Many obstacles we face seem overwhelming because they seem too large to manage. Chunk the obstacle down into smaller pieces that you can overcome one step at a time. After all, every journey begins with a single, small step.

Sometimes, once you try all of your methods for overcoming obstacles, an obstacle is still insurmountable. That's okay. When you cannot overcome an obstacle, it is important to reevaluate and set a new goal that allows you to keep moving forward.

HOPEFUL MINDS LESSON TWO: Positive Feelings and Smart Actions

📖 Additional Resources for Educators

- SMART Goals: How to Make Your Goals Achievable
- The 90 Second Rule You Can't Afford to Ignore
- The Neuroanatomical Transformation of the Teenage Brain: Jill Bolte Taylor
- Experiencing and Expressing Emotion
- Achieving Your Goals: An Evidence-Based Approach
- Zimbabwe Friendship Bench
- Voices Around the World
- Magic Johnson Biography

*Links to resources can be found on Page 116

LESSON 2 OVERVIEW

Total Instruction Time: 45 Minutes

FORMAT

Instructor Reading and Discussion
My Hopework Book Worksheets
Instructor Reading and Discussion
My Hopework Book Worksheets
Hope Hero Spotlight

LESSON OBJECTIVES

Understand the Value of Feelings
Understand the Two Ingredients of Hope:
Positive Feelings and Smart Actions

PRINT-OUTS FOR EDUCATORS

Classroom Hope Sunflower Center & Petals (from Lesson 1)
SMART Goals Visual (optional)

PRINT-OUTS FOR STUDENTS

Feelings Chart (My Hopework Book Page 13)
Feelings Worksheet (My Hopework Book Page 14)
My Brain (My Hopework Book page 15)
SMART Goals (My Hopework Book Page 16)
Inspired Actions (My Hopework Book page 17)

LESSON 2 OUTLINE

	10 Minutes	Lesson 1 Review
	10 Minutes	"What are Feelings and Why Do They Matter?" Educator Reading
	10 Minutes	My Hopework Book: Feelings Worksheet and My Brain
	5 Minutes	"Smart Actions and Goals" Educator Reading
	5 Minutes	My Hopework Book: Smart Goals Worksheet
	5 Minutes	Hope Hero Spotlight: Magic Johnson
	Remaining	Final Discussion (Optional)

HOPEFUL MINDS LESSON TWO: Positive Feelings and Smart Actions

LESSON 2 PREPARATION

Prior to the lesson, prepare the following materials:

- Print out your classroom Hope Sunflower Petals if not completed during Lesson 1.
- Print out Happiness Habits and SMART Goals visuals for your classroom (optional)
- Print out Hopework Book worksheets for students

LESSON 1 REVIEW
10 Minutes

Discuss the following questions with your class:

- Can someone review our classroom definition of hope?
- Can someone share their personal definition of hope?
- Why is hope important in all we do?
- What are the Five Keys to Shine Hope?
- What are some feeling words you think of when you think of hope?

LESSON 1 REVIEW CNT'D

- Why is it important to notice that we didn't always react the same way as our classmates?
- Did you see anyone who acted out the same emotion you did but in a different way (e.g. they showed anger by yelling but you showed anger by stomping your feet)?
- Why is it important that we all show our emotions differently?

It's important for students to begin to understand that we all react differently and that's okay- there is not one right way to react. However, we need to understand how someone else might react so that we can respond appropriately with understanding or what we call empathy.

Make sure to point out that even when we felt the same emotion, we didn't always react the same way. It's important to see that not everyone will react the same way you do.

IDENTIFYING FEELINGS
10 Minutes

Discuss the following questions with your class:
- What is the purpose of emotions?
- How can we identify what emotions we are feeling?

Read the following to your students:

Now that we know how to identify our feelings, we need to learn what to do when we have feelings. It's really important that we learn how to react in a smart way.

Let's talk about what we should do when we feel a new emotion.

The first thing we should do is listen to our body and brain to figure out which emotion we are feeling. What emotions are you feeling right now?

Once we know what we are feeling, then we need to determine if it's a positive feeling or a negative feeling. Who remembers what the two ingredients for hope are? *(Answer: Positive feelings and smart actions)*

HOPEFUL MINDS LESSON TWO: Positive Feelings and Smart Actions

IDENTIFYING FEELINGS CNT'D

That's right! We want to make sure that we are listening to all of our feelings, but getting to our positive feelings and releasing the energy from our negative feelings so that we can stay hopeful.
Do you remember what we do when we feel a negative emotion, like fear or anger? *(Answer: Use our Stress Skills to calm down)*

That's right! You can think about your fear or anger like a little ball of fire in your chest. When we are in our downstairs brain, we feed that ball of energy and make it bigger and bigger, just like adding wood to a fire. However, what happens when you stop putting wood on the fire?

When you stop putting wood on a fire, it eventually loses its energy and burns out. When we take the time to calm down when we are angry or scared, we are releasing the energy the same way that we let the energy leave a fire- we're just doing it much quicker. We listen to what the feelings tell us, but we don't act out.

For instance, if someone calls you a name on the playground what would you feel? *(Example responses: Angry, sad, scared, etc.)*

For instance, if someone calls you a name on the playground what would you feel? *(Example responses: Angry, sad, scared, etc.)*

Right! And if you act right away while you are still in your downstairs brain and feeling angry / sad / afraid, you might punch them. Or call them a name back. What would happen if you did that? *(Acknowledge student answers)*

You both get in trouble. Your real power is in being able to breathe through the anger / fear / sadness. Not act, just breathe through it. Walk away. Listen to what the feelings are telling you, and letting the "energy" from your negative feelings go away.

Once the energy is released, you can make a smart decision. What might you do to resolve the problem? *(Acknowledge student answers)*

IDENTIFYING FEELINGS CNT'D

IDENTIFYING FEELINGS CNT'D

That is right, and that is where your power is. See, other people have upstairs and downstairs brains as well. If they call names, they are in their downstairs brain. Don't let them convince you to join them. Your power is in your upstairs brain.

Once you find ways to stay there, you will have real power.

We can also use our upstairs brain to help us create positive feelings once we've released the negative ones. Positive feelings are not always "good" feelings; they are any feelings that help us have hope.

FEELINGS WORKSHEET AND MY BRAIN WORKSHEET
MY HOPEWORK BOOK PAGE 14-15
10 Minutes

Have the students turn to My Hopework Book Page 14 (Feelings Worksheet). Help students find ways to identify where they feel their feelings, what their feelings tell them, and what to do when we feel them. Have students use the Feelings Chart on My Hopework Book Page 13 as a reference.

Then, have students move to page 14 and practice labeling emotions that occur in the upper brain and lower brain. Encourage them to think about where they feel emotions associated with the upper and lower brain and color in the areas on the bottom of the page.

Let students be creative with these activities. The goal is not perfect grammar or drawings; the goal is to have students start independently thinking about what they feel and where they feel it in their bodies.

HOPEFUL MINDS LESSON TWO: Positive Feelings and Smart Actions

INSPIRED ACTIONS AND SMART GOALS
5 Minutes

Read the following to your students:

What is the second ingredient of hope? Inspired actions!

Inspired actions are also the Third Key to Shine Hope. They are hope tools that help us keep our hope strong all the time. Inspired actions help us reach our goals, stay physically and mentally healthy, and increase our hope and hope skills. One of the best inspired action tools we have is creating SMART goals.

Goals are important because they give us something to look forward to and to work towards. We can enjoy the steps we take to reach our goal and feel a sense of accomplishment along the way.

What is a goal you have? *(Acknowledge student responses)*

Emphasize that goals and wishes are different. Goals are things that the students can achieve through their own persistence and hard work.

In order to use our goals as hope tools, we must set smart, realistic goals. For example, you don't want to just say "I want to be the best basketball player in the world." Instead, we want to set smaller goals that will help you get there. What are some goals you could set that would help you become a better basketball player? *(Example responses: learn to dribble with my left hand, improve my free throw shot, learn how to throw a bounce pass, etc.)*

When we are aiming towards a goal, it makes us feel hopeful and motivated. It is important that we always have goals that we are aiming for.

HOPEFUL MINDS LESSON TWO: Positive Feelings and Smart Actions

INSPIRED ACTIONS WORKSHEET
MY HOPEWORK BOOK PAGE 17
10 Minutes

Have the students turn to My Hopework Book Page 17 (Inspired Actions Worksheet) and give students the following instructions:

Raise your hand if you want good grades this quarter.

Well, we can help ourselves get good grades by setting smart goals for ourselves. On this worksheet, I want each of you to pick one goal you have for the classroom. It should be something that you can accomplish this week that will help you do better in school.

Have the students fill in the Inspired Actions Worksheet. If they need help, students can refer to the SMART Goals visual on My Hopework Book Page 16.

Help the students pick small goals that they can accomplish in the next week or two. Goals can be academically-based *(for example, "I want to do extra math problems to prepare for our quiz" or "I want to read three chapters of my book by Friday")* or they can be behavioral-based *(for example "I won't lose recess time for talking during class this week" or "I will keep my desk clean all week")*.

The goal of this activity is to help students begin to identify the small steps they can take to move towards their larger goals.

HOPEFUL MINDS LESSON TWO: Positive Feelings and Smart Actions

HOPE HERO SPOTLIGHT
MAGIC JOHNSON
5 Minutes

Read the following story out loud to the students. Encourage the students to identify what Magic Johnson was hopeful for and how he took actions to achieve his goals.

Who here has heard of Magic Johnson? *(Show picture for reference if necessary)*

Earvin "Magic" Johnson was one of the best NBA basketball players of all time. He wasn't always successful though- there were lots of times when bad things happened and he felt angry or sad. However, Magic Johnson was able to use hope and smart actions to continue to pursue his dreams.

Magic Johnson had 9 brothers and sisters. He had to spend a lot of time taking care of them and couldn't play basketball whenever he wanted to. How do you think it made Magic Johnson feel that he couldn't play basketball when we wanted to? *(Acknowledge students responses)*

But Magic Johnson knew that he wanted to be in the NBA. So he released his negative emotions and focused on his smart actions - he kept a positive attitude and he used smart actions; he wanted to be a good player at basketball, he saw progress by his baskets made, he set times he could practice, he found good mentors to help him, and he kept on track. He kept track of how he was doing and set himself up for success even though he had many challenges.

By working hard on his hope skills and his basketball skills, Magic Johnson was able to play basketball in college, and even the LA Lakers with the NBA. During his second season, he hurt his knee really badly and missed 45 games.

How do you think he felt when he couldn't play because he was hurt? *(Acknowledge student responses)*

He said that it was the saddest he's ever felt. However, he knew that he couldn't respond with his lower brain. So Magic Johnson used his Happiness Habits and hope to keep himself positive. And keep setting new smart goals. And it worked! He was able to go back and play for ten more years.

Ten years after he hurt his knee, Magic Johnson got a bad disease. He realized that because of his disease, he couldn't play basketball anymore. He was so sad and angry!

HOPE HERO SPOTLIGHT CNT'D

But he knew that focusing on that sadness and anger wasn't good. So instead, he decided he needed to change his goals, and add good feelings and smart actions! Magic Johnson realized that this was an opportunity for him to do something new and exciting. He decided he wanted to help other people so he started schools to help kids.

Magic Johnson is proof that if you work on your hope skills, you can achieve your dreams, and even sometimes dreams have to change, and that is OK. Science tells us that life is all about enjoying the journey to the destination, not reaching the destination. So we have to be willing to change, no matter what life brings.*

*This story was created from publicly available information. It does not suggest endorsement of Hopeful Minds, or any affiliation by known celebrity to our program. All information is for illustrative purposes for youth, to demonstrate skills used to create, maintain, and grow hope.

FINAL DISCUSSION

Discuss the following questions with your class:

- What are the two main ingredients of hope?
- Can you see how Magic Johnson used positive feelings to overcome obstacles?
- What is an example of how Magic Johnson used smart actions instead of responding with his lower brain?

ADDITIONAL ACTIVITIES FOR HOME OR VIRTUAL LEARNING

Consider using the following Hopework activities to help students enhance their hope skills:

- Reading facial expressions can help us understand what others are feeling. Take breaks during virtual learning to let students show off their best feeling faces. How do you show that you are happy/sad/mad? How is your face different from your classmates'?
- Use 5 minute yoga breaks to help students practice Stress Skills and stay active during virtual learning.

HAPPINESS HABITS

Directions: Circle your top four favorite happiness habits from the list below. If there are additional happiness habits you use that are not on the list, use the space below the add them.

- Utilizing strengths
- Pursuing passion
- Activating purpose
- Smiling
- Exercising
- Playing or Listening to Music
- Spending time in Nature
- Showing Gratitude and Kindness
- Playing Games
- Volunteering
- Time with Family and Friends
- Experiencing Wonder & Awe
- Practicing Faith
- Sleeping
- Nutrition
- Dancing and Singing
- Donating
- Giving a hug
- Setting Goals
- Practicing Affirmations

My favorite happiness habits:

-
-
-
-
-
-

S.M.A.R.T. GOALS

Specific
Be specific about your goal. Think about these questions when creating your goal: What needs to be accomplished? Who is responsible for it? What steps will you take to achieve it?

Measurable
Can you measure your progress? If this goal will take a long time to achieve, set shorter term goals to reach along the way.

Achievable
Are you inspired and motivated to reach your goal? Do you have the tools or skills you need? If not, do you know how you can get them?

Relevant
Does your goal make sense? Does it go along with what you are trying to achieve in the bigger picture?

Time-bound
Is your timing realistic? Can you achieve your goal in the time period set? Think about what you may want to achieve at the halfway point.

HAPPINESS HABITS

Happiness Habits are healthy, long-term actions that cause your brain to release happiness hormones including endorphins, dopamine, serotonin, and oxytocin. Happiness Habits help you stay in your upstairs brain, where you access the problem-solving skills, collaboration, and passion critical for hope.

Positive Feelings

Positive feelings, the first ingredient of hope, are feelings that are located in your upstairs brain like wonder, joy, and peace that make it easier to overcome obstacles that get in the way of hope. You proactively manage the emotional despair of hopelessness using Stress Skills and use your Happiness Habits to stay in your upstairs brain, where you then energetically move towards your goals in life.

- **Activating purpose**
- **Pursuing passion**
- **Utilizing strengths**
- **Meditation**
- **Smiling**
- **Exercising / Nutrition**
- **Creating / listening to music**
- **Dancing / Singing**
- **Drawing / Painting**
- **Gratitude**
- **Volunteering**
- **Wonder/Awe**
- **Quality sleep**
- **Doodling**

© The Shine Hope Company, LLC

INSPIRED ACTIONS

Inspired Actions, the second ingredient of hope, are the deliberate steps you take toward your goals in life. Inspired Actions help you to move away from the motivational helplessness, the second ingredient of hopelessness, and toward what you are hopeful for in life.

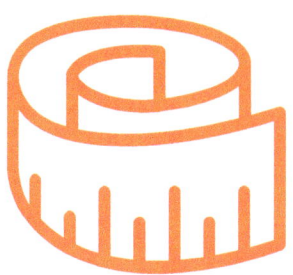

Types of Goals:

WOOP	SMART
Achievement	Stretch
Intrinsic	Micro-Goals

Pathways, Agency, and Regoaling

Obstacles are inevitable, and sometimes you can't reach the goal as you intended. It is important to embrace obstacles to goals, learn to pivot or reevaluate, be flexible and adaptable, and never be afraid to ask for help.

If a goal seems too big, use the stepping process or create micro-goals to chunk it down into smaller goals. Think of one thing you can do in the next 20 minutes. And know when you need to re-goal.

© The Shine Hope Company, LLC

"All kids need is a little help, a little hope and somebody who believes in them."

– Magic Johnson

LESSON THREE

Challenges to Hope

"I want people to feel hope and to know you will come out the other side stronger and a better version of yourself."

-Selena Gomez

LESSON THREE
CHALLENGES TO HOPE

THE IMPORTANCE OF SOCIAL CONNECTION

Social connection, when you feel close to other people, is essential for hope. Scientific evidence suggests that social connection is as necessary for us as food and water. We know that it is critical that every person has at least one person they can connect with regularly.

The importance of social connection in our lives is evident in the way we communicate: our facial expressions, intonations, and sense of touch have all evolved to allow us to form relationships with others. Strong social connections can improve our physical and mental health. Research has shown that a strong social connection strengthens your immune system, helps you recover from disease, lengthens your life, lowers anxiety and depression, and increases self-esteem, empathy, and hope.

Luckily, social connection isn't just about physical closeness. We can experience social connections even if we are physically isolated. Social connection is based on your subjective feeling of connection and can be fostered through compassion, volunteering, and spending time with your family and friends.

YOUR HOPE NETWORK

The Fourth Key to Shine Hope is your **Nourishing Network**, made up of family members, friends, neighbors, mentors, children, doctors, clergy, teachers, or even pets. Anyone who you can turn to when you are feeling hopeless belongs in your Hope Network. You need to trust them, and they need to be positive influences in your life.

The people that you surround yourself with aren't always the people that should be in your Hope Network. When you set up your Hope Network, it is important to surround yourself with people that encourage you to be in your upstairs brain. In fact, did you know that your friends influence your weight, habits, and happiness? It is therefore important to make sure they are influencing you in positive ways.

As you begin to think about your Hope Network, know that, like hope, your Hope Network is not set in stone. As people come in and out of your life, your Hope Network will grow and change. So, if you cannot think of many people for your Hope Network now, that is okay. You can set a SMART goal to continue adding healthy people to your Hope Network, and cultivating the network.

It is critical to not just have a Nourishing Network but to cultivate your network. Relationships take work, time, and energy. Oftentimes when we feel alone, we tend to withdraw, yet that can create more aloneness. What we need to learn to do is reach out, and continue to foster these relationships. Strengthen your Hope Network by actively working on your relationships with the people within your network.

It is also important to understand the importance of health versus unhealthy relationships by recognizing the signs of unhealthy relationships. Check out this article on Psych Central on the signs of toxic relationships (https://psychcentral.com/relationships/signs-of-toxic-relationships). It is true with friends, too. Look at this article in Psychology Today about 8 signs of a toxic friendship.

You can enhance your Hope Network with:

5:1 Rule: In healthy relationships, like the ones you should have with the people in your Hope Network, you should exchange five positive comments for every critical one. You may find that using this ratio is harder than it seems. Like everything else we do in this course, the 5:1 rule may take practice to achieve.

Empathy: The empathy you give and receive from the relationships with the people around you provides an emotional connection and support system while reducing your feelings of worry, stress, loneliness, and hopelessness.

Kindness: When you perform an act of kindness, it not only bolsters your hope; it also positively affects the hope of the person on the receiving end, and the hope of anyone who witnesses it. These acts of kindness also enhance your relationships with people within your Hope Network.

Compassion, Forgiveness, and Self-Forgiveness: Forgiveness is one of the key ways that you show empathy to the people around you. Forgiveness is when you release the negative emotions, such as anger, sadness, or frustration, that are associated with an action that another person (or your former self) has made. Forgiveness is larger than simply saying, "it's okay" when someone apologizes; it is a conscious decision to release the negative emotions and return to a hopeful mindset.

Lastly, everyone experiences a breakup in their lifetime, and navigating breakups, whether with a friend or a significant other, can bring up difficult emotions. Breakups disrupt routines and challenge the preference for consistency, making it a challenging experience. Breakups can also bring up hopelessness and subsequent anxiety and depression. Learning how to manage breakups in a healthy way allows you to move from hopelessness to hope.

To manage breakups in a healthy way, remember to use your Stress Skills as you navigate the emotions that arise from the break up. Find your healthy Nourishing Network and talk through your thoughts and feelings about the breakup, and find a way to gain a sense of closure.

CHALLENGES TO HOPE

The Fifth Key to Shine Hope is **Eliminating Challenges**, which are generally around negative thinking patterns that get in the way of our ability to hope; limiting beliefs, ANTS (Automatic Negative Thoughts), worry, rumination, focusing on uncontrollables, and internalizing failure. When you experience these challenges to hope, they cause your body to go through the 90-second physiological stress response.

When you identify the challenge to hope that you are facing, it makes it easier for you to use your Stress Skills, Happiness Habits, Inspired Actions, and your Nourishing Network to manage the challenge and return to a hopeful mindset. It is therefore important to learn how to identify each of the challenges to hope and what to do when you encounter them.

CHALLENGE #1: LIMITING BELIEFS

Our beliefs are powerful forces that influence the direction of our lives, so it's easy to see how limiting beliefs can drastically influence our success. Limiting beliefs are at the core of our anxieties, fears, and insecurities. In order to truly create, maintain, and grow hope over your life, you must first identify the limiting beliefs you have around hope and find ways to overcome them.

CHALLENGE #2: ANTS (AUTOMATIC NEGATIVE THOUGHTS)

Every time you have a negative thought, your brain releases chemicals. The key is to start identifying these thoughts and challenging them. One great method for preventing ANTS is by switching to "Yes, and…" thinking. When you are presented with a scenario, such as being invited to a party, it can be easy to immediately respond with "yes, but…" in your mind. This immediately allows ANTS to enter your thought process. Instead, when presented with an opportunity, try the classic improv technique of "yes, and…". With "yes… and" thinking, you are allowing yourself to instead focus on positive outcomes:

As you go through your day, work on replacing your ANTS with positive, self-affirming thoughts.

CHALLENGE #3: ALL-OR-NOTHING THINKING

All-or-nothing thinking is a negative thought pattern in which you only think in extremes. Rather than seeing yourself or your experiences in shades of gray, you place everything in black and white. Rather than seeing all of the solutions to a problem, all-or-nothing thinking forces you to only see either complete success or complete failure.

When you start to hear yourself use absolute terms like "never" or "always," it's important to take some deep breaths and use a Stress Skill to return to your upstairs brain. Once you are back in your upstairs brain, you can replace those all-or-nothing thoughts with positive thoughts.

CHALLENGE #4: RUMINATION

Rumination refers to when you repeatedly go over a thought or a problem from your past in your head, without end.

The habit of ruminating can be detrimental to your mental health. Rumination is associated with numerous negative mental states, including depression, anxiety, post-traumatic stress disorder, and hopelessness.

Once you identify that you are ruminating or that you have entered a rumination cycle, it is important to take a 90-second pause, then use a Stress Skill to return to your upstairs brain. Once there, use your Happiness Habits to stay in your upstairs brain and ensure you don't return to your rumination.

CHALLENGE #5: WORRY

Worry is when you feel anxious or afraid about real or imagined future scenarios. Where rumination focuses on the past, worry focuses on the future. Worry forces you to fixate on and respond to the future dangers that you think you may encounter. Excessive worrying takes a toll on your emotional strength, makes it difficult to concentrate, and can lead to hopelessness.

Worrying is natural, and in small doses, it isn't unhealthy. Letting yourself worry briefly about the future can help you to acknowledge your feelings and prepare for the things that you are worried about. However, once you have identified and accepted the negative feelings associated with your worry, it is important that you learn to let them, as well as the worry, go using Stress Skills.

CHALLENGE #6: FOCUSING ON UNCONTROLLABLES

Think back to the things you were worried about yesterday or today. How many of the things were within your control? For most people, the things they worry and ruminate about the most are the things that they cannot control.

When you worry about things you cannot control, you create hopelessness cycles that you cannot use inspired actions to overcome. These cycles impact both your mental health and your hope. If you want to have a strong, hopeful mindset, you have to learn to release negative emotions associated with the things you cannot control.

CHALLENGE #7: INTERNALIZING FAILURE

One of the biggest threats to our hopeful mindsets is failure. When we experience failure, we often experience feelings of despair and a sense of helplessness (the two ingredients of hopelessness). If allowed to run unchecked, this negative feeling and sense of inaction has the power to pull us out of our upstairs brain, into our downstairs brain, and into a cycle of hopelessness.

When you are in your downstairs brain, your goals seem tougher, and you cannot use the positive feelings, inspired actions, and problem-solving skills in your upstairs brains. As a result, when you internalize a failure, you are then more likely to experience more failure in the future.

To overcome this biological response and hopelessness cycle, the key is to learn how to not internalize failure. See, failure is an indication that something in your process failed, not that you failed. And once you learn to deconstruct the process, you can end failure.

CONTINUING YOUR HOPE JOURNEY

Hope is a thought and an action that takes practice. Like any other skill, hope skills must be practiced daily, activated, and practiced more. The more you practice, the easier it gets, and the more the Hopeful Mindset becomes an instinctual part of your daily life.

Today, we are going to talk about the resources you can use to continue your own hope journey, further activate hope in your classroom, and begin spreading hope to your school and your community:

Write Your Own Hope Story: Now that you have the skills to create, maintain, and grow hope, your hope journey is up to you. Decide how you want to inspire hope in yourself and others, and then use your positive feelings and inspired actions to make it a reality.

Sponsor a Hopeful Minds Event: Work with your Campus Activities Committee to sponsor an event that helps your fellow classmates learn hope skills and embrace their own hopeful mindsets.

Continue Teaching Hope: We developed Hopeful Minds so you can teach hope to others. Download our other curriculums and continue teaching hope in your local schools, Boys and Girls Club, YMCA, church, and more. To continue exploring the Hopeful Minds curriculums today, visit www.hopefulminds.org/hopeful-minds-curriculums/

Measure Hope: Take time each week to have your students complete the Children's Snyder Hope Scale (with parent permission). This scale will help them monitor their hope levels and allow you to connect with students that may need extra support from you and the other members of their Hope Network.

Hang Posters for Hope: Put up posters and signs so that others can find the Science of Hope and start activating it in their own lives. Our resources are available at no cost for all here: www.hopefulcities.org/hang-posters-for-hope/

Create a Hope Initiative at your School: How can your school more successfully help students move from hopelessness to hope? Student-run initiatives are a great way to influence positive change and will help your students activate hope in their own lives while they spread hope to their community.

Put up Yard Signs for Hope: Yard Signs can be placed in your yard or your window to share the message of hope with your community. The purpose of the sign is to spread the message of the power of hope and encourage people to start learning about hope and using hope tools. By putting up a sign, you may inspire someone to take the challenge, seek therapy, teach hope to kids, or practice skills. Every action for hope counts in ways that are often unseen. All of our yard signs are available for download and available for purchase at CafePress: www.hopefulcities.org/put-up-yard-signs-for-hope/

Get Support: Everyone needs help sometimes, and it is so important to be proactive about your hope: www.hopefulcities.org/get-support

Plant a Sunflower Garden for Hope: We use the sunflower as the global symbol for hope. We encourage you to plant a garden at your school, to grow sunflowers on your classroom windowsills, or to give students sunflower seeds so that they can grow their own flowers at home. You can practice Shine Hope skills as you plant, as well. Hope is always better when shared. Find out more here: www.hopefulcities.org/plant-a-sunflower-garden-for-hope/

It's important to remember that the hope journey is not over when you finish this curriculum. You and your students now have the skills you need to create, maintain, and grow hope; however, it is up to you to keep practicing the Five Keys to Shine Hope. Going forward, one of the most important things you can do is continue to use hope resources so that you can activate hope in your life, as well as in the lives of your students and your community.

Continue to find the signs of hope that are all around you. Pay attention to the small moments that inspire your positive feelings, like smiling at a stranger or enjoying a quiet moment in nature. Embrace the big moments that nurture your hopeful mindset, like when you meet someone you know will be a huge part of your life or when you watch the people you love achieve their dreams. Even in the midst of hopelessness, our lives are made up of millions of moments of hope.

HOPEFUL MINDS LESSON THREE: Challenges to Hope

 Additional Resources for Educators

- CDC: Violence Prevention - Adverse Childhood Experiences
- 9 Types of Hopelessness and How to Overcome Them
- ACEs Aware
- Big Brothers, Big Sisters
- Welcoming Schools
- Selena Gomez Biography

*Links to resources can be found on Page 117

HOPEFUL MINDS LESSON THREE: Challenges to Hope

LESSON 3 OVERVIEW
Total Instruction Time: 45 Minutes

FORMAT
Instructor Reading and Discussion
My Hopework Book Worksheet
Instructor Reading and Discussion
Activity: Break the Worry Cycle
My Hopework Book Worksheets
Hope Hero Spotlight

LESSON OBJECTIVES
Identify Challenges to Hope, including Worry and Hopelessness
Establish Strategies to overcome challenges
Develop a Hope Network

PRINT-OUTS FOR EDUCATORS
Nourishing Network Visual (optional)
Eliminating Challenges Visual (optional)
Certified Hope Ambassador Certificate (optional)
Hope Emoji Worksheet Five Keys to Shine Hope Worksheet

PRINT-OUTS FOR STUDENTS
Nourishing Network (My Hopework Book Page 19)
Hope Supervillains (My Hopework Book Page 20)
My Hope Hero (My Hopework Book Page 21)
Control the Controllables (My Hopework Book Page 22)
Hope Worksheet (My Hopework Book Page 23; optional)
What Fuels my Hope (My Hopework Book Page 24; optional)
What am I Hopeful For? (My Hopework Book Page 25; optional)

LESSON 3 OUTLINE

📖	5 Minutes	"The Importance of the Hope Network" Educator Reading
📄	5 Minutes	My Hopework Book: Hope Network Worksheet
📖	5 Minutes	"Challenges to Hope" Educator Reading and Class Discussion
📄	5 Minutes	Activity: Break the Worry Cycle
📄	10 Minutes	My Hopework Book: Hope Supervillain Worksheet, Hope Hero, & Control the Uncontrollables
📓	5 Minutes	Hope Hero Spotlight: Selena Gomez
📖	5 Minutes	Final Hope Thoughts
💬	Remaining	Hope Ambassador Celebration

LESSON 3 PREPARATION

Prior to the lesson, prepare the following materials:

- Print the visuals and worksheets included at the end of this lesson.
- Prepare Hope Ambassador Certificates for each of your students.

IMPORTANCE OF HOPE NETWORK
5 Minutes

Read the following to your students:

We've learned that hope is an important skill. When we use hope, we can do better in school, health, life and sports. We can take our negative emotions, release them, and instead focus on positive emotions and smart actions.

We can think of hope like a superhero that is helping us succeed. The more we work on our hope skills, the stronger our hope superhero will be.

However, like all superheroes, hope also has supervillains that it has to fight. Anything that makes us lose hope, like bad feelings or challenges, are hope supervillains. Today, we are going to talk about some of the supervillains that battle our hope.

By far the biggest supervillain that our hope faces is hopelessness. When we experience hopelessness, we feel weak and feel like we should give up. Hopelessness is a negative feeling of despair, and a sense of helplessness, or like we can't act. Like someone took our power away. Can you think of a time when you felt hopeless?

- What other feelings did you experience when you felt hopeless?
- What did you think you couldn't do? Where was your power?

Hopelessness experience we have in life. We might even feel it many times a day! Like if someone cuts, says something mean, or we get a bad grade, or if we trip and fall. Sometimes, things can just feel like they are 'too big' or 'too much.' Think of a time when you felt hopelessness: What are some other feelings you had when you were feeling hopelessness? *(Acknowledge students responses)*

HOPEFUL MINDS LESSON THREE: Challenges to Hope

IMPORTANCE OF HOPE NETWORK CNT'D

That is okay. When we feel hopeless, we can fight hopelessness with hope.

When our hope is overwhelmed by hopelessness, we can use our strongest defense: our Hope Network. When you feel hopelessness, focus on your deep breathing and your Happiness Habits. Try to use your skills to first change your emotions to hope. Then use your smart actions to come up with goals that will help fight the hopelessness. Start with one tiny, tiny step.

Sometimes, we feel hopeless because we cannot change something. So it is important to think about it - do we have power? What is in our control in the situation? Is anything? It is important to focus on what we can control, otherwise we are sure to experience hopelessness. When the world around us is scary, it is easy to feel hopeless. When we feel hopelessness over things we cannot change, it can help to focus on things bigger than ourselves, like our faith or things in the natural world that fill us with wonder. It can help us realize that no one has all the answers and everyone has moments like these. We can use our hope skills to give our problems over to the big, wide universe, and have faith that things will work out.

However, sometimes even with all our hope skills, our hopelessness or worry is just too strong for us to fight all by ourselves. Luckily, our hope isn't the only superhero on our side.

The Fourth Key to Shine Hope is your Nourishing Network, or Hope Network. Your Hope Network is the group of people around you who know you, appreciate you, see your strengths, and help you keep your hopeful attitude. People in your Hope Network can help your hope fight hopelessness. Can you think of people who are in your Hope Network? *(Acknowledge students responses)*

Connections with other people make us stronger. While many of us may want to hide when we have challenges, the reality is that a good, strong Hope Network can help us get through tough times. But they can only help you if you let them know that you and your hope need help!

When you are feeling overwhelmed by hopelessness, the most important thing you can do is to reach out to someone in your Hope Network and ask for help. We must really think about who we have in our Hope Network, keep these relationships strong, and reach out to them not just in good times, but in times of need.

IMPORTANCE OF HOPE NETWORK CNT'D

NOURISHING NETWORK WORKSHEET
MY HOPEWORK BOOK PAGE 19
5 Minutes

Have the students turn to My Hopework Book Page 19 (Nourishing Network Worksheet). Help students think of people to put in their Hope Networks:

People in your Hope Network can include family members, teachers, friends, neighbors, mentors, big brothers/big sisters, doctors, or even pets! Anyone who you can turn to when you are feeling hopeless belongs in your Hope Network. We need to trust them, and they need to be positive influences in our lives.

Sometimes we don't feel good because something is actually wrong with us. Do you remember how we talked about biology in lesson one? Our biology impacts how we feel, and how we feel impacts our biology. Therefore, it's important you also add your doctors to your Hope Network. If you don't have a doctor to put down yet, that's okay. Next time you go to the doctor, you can talk to them about being in your Hope Network!

And if you don't have anyone in your Hope Network that is okay because you can now use your hope skills to start creating a Hope Network. Who would you like to be in it? How can you feel good about it, and start taking smart actions? *(Acknowledge students responses)*

While completing Nourishing Network worksheets, educate students about mental health resources at their school and in the community. If students cannot come up with someone in their Hope Network, it is vital that teachers fulfill that role and let students know they are there to support them.

Consider creating a Hope Network bulletin board in your classroom where students can share the important people in their own Hope Network. Having a Hope Network where students can see it is a great way to continue to remind them that there are always people around when they feel alone.

HOPEFUL MINDS LESSON THREE: Challenges to Hope

CHALLENGES TO HOPE
5 Minutes

Read the following to your students:

The Fifth Key to Shine Hope is **Eliminating Challenges**. Challenges are all of the supervillains that our hope must face. Like hopelessness, these other challenges have the potential to harm our hope.

However, we can use our Stress Skills, Happiness Habits, Inspired Actions, and Nourishing Networks to keep our hope strong and make sure we can overcome any challenge.
Today, we are going to talk about two more of the hope supervillains you might face. Let's talk about failure. What is failure? *(Acknowledge student responses)*

Everyone fails at something at some point in their life. Maybe you miss a goal when you're playing soccer. Maybe you get a bad grade on a test. Maybe you did poorly during your recital.
It's important to remember that we all fail. Failure is a part of life. Failing at something doesn't make us a failure. It just means that one of the steps on the way to our goal failed. It does NOT mean that we, personally, are failures.

Do you understand the difference? *(Acknowledge student responses)*

Say you missed the goal, it doesn't mean you are a failure, it just means that you need to practice more. If you got a bad grade on a test, it means you might need to study more next time or find someone to help you study. Failing at something means our way to that 'something' failed, not that we as a person are failures.

In fact, failing can even be a good thing as long as we have hope! Does anyone know how failing can be a good thing? *(Acknowledge students responses)*

Failing is how we learn. It is the thing that keeps us working hard and improving. When we fail, it allows us to use our hope to become an even better version of ourselves. And we, as humans, always need to keep learning and growing. It is what makes life fun.

The second supervillain our hope must face is worry. Who knows what worry is? Where do you feel it in your body? *(Acknowledge students responses)*

CHALLENGES TO HOPE CNT'D

When we face bad or scary things in our lives, we tend to worry about them. When we are worrying about something, we are not present and in the moment. We are thinking about what may or may not happen. And so much of what may or may not happen is out of our control. We can only 'control the controllables.

When we are feeling worried, we can help hope fight it. We fight worry by focusing on where we are right now. When we use our senses to focus on where we are right now, we stop thinking about the thing we are worrying about.

BREAK THE WORRY CYCLE
10 Minutes

Review the five senses:

- Sight
- Smell
- Touch
- Taste
- Sound

Have students sit quietly in their chairs for 30 seconds. Have them use their five senses to take in the world around them. Encourage them to identify something for each sense.

- What did you see?
- What did you smell?
- What did you touch?
- What did you taste?
- What did you hear?

Now, can you be worried and describe a picture at the same time? No! Can you be worried and smell something at the same time? No! By focusing on your five senses, you can focus on the present, get out of your mind, and let go of your worries, and the things you can't control.

We can also do this when we encounter the hope supervillain **"rumination."** It is when we think over and over and over about something that happened in the past. While it is important to reflect on what we have done, and take action if we need, we can't change the past.

Would you watch a bad TV show over and over and over? *(Acknowledge students responses)*

HOPEFUL MINDS LESSON THREE: Challenges to Hope

BREAK THE WORRY CYCLE CNT'D

No, you would change the channel of the TV! We must be proactive about changing the 'channel' in our mind, and getting back to the present. Again, you can do this with your senses.

When you are present, you are less likely to have accidents as well! The more hopeful we are, the more engaged in the present moment. And the more aware of what is around you. When you are worrying in your mind, you aren't paying attention, so you might do something like trip in the hall, run into something with your bike, or even walk into a pole!

Has anyone ever done that? Were you alert and aware, or carried away by something in your head? Can you see how hope even impacts your safety, and well being? *(Acknowledge students responses)*

HOPE SUPERVILLAIN, MY HOPE SUPERHERO WORKSHEET, & CONTROL THE UNCONTROLLABLES
MY HOPEWORK BOOK PAGE 20-22
10 Minutes

Have the students turn to My Hopework Book Page 20 (Hope Supervillain Worksheet). Encourage students to get creative as they draw their hope supervillains and monsters. Help students identify the challenges to hope they are currently facing. Then have students turn to My Hopework Book Page 21 and have them draw and write about their hope hero. Encourage them to describe what makes their chosen person a hope hero.

Then, have students complete the "Control the Controllables" Worksheet (My Hopework Book Page 22) to identify stressors associated with school and the pandemic. Have students write things they can control inside of the sunflower, and things they cannot control outside of the sunflower. Encouraging students to focus on what they can control and release what we cannot control can help them stay in a hopeful mindset.

- Things they can control might include: Wearing a mask, washing their hands, completing their school work on time, being kind, expressing their feelings, and asking for help when they need it.

- Things they cannot control might include: Getting sick, their parents getting sick, bullying, virtual learning or classroom safety precautions, their parents or teachers feeling stressed, how long the pandemic will last, and the actions of others.

HOPE HERO HIGHLIGHT
SELENA GOMEZ
5 Minutes

Read the following to your students:

Who knows who Selena Gomez is? *(Show her photo for reference)*

Selena Gomez is an actress and singer. As an actress, she is most well known for her time on Disney Channel, where she played Alex Russo on Wizards of Waverly Place. She also started singing while she was on Disney Channel, and is now one of the most popular pop musicians in America. Have any of you seen Selena Gomez on TV or heard her songs? *(Acknowledge student answers)*

However, Selena Gomez has had to face all of the hope supervillains throughout her life. In 2014, Selena was diagnosed with lupus. Lupus is a disease that causes someone's immune system to attack their own body.

Selena's lupus caused her physical pain; it hurt her stomach, made her skin break out in rashes, and made her hands and feet swell and throb. It also gave her anxiety, panic attacks, and depression. The lupus got worse, and Selena's kidneys began to shut down.

Her doctors told her that if she couldn't find someone to give her a kidney, she would die. How do you think Selena felt at that moment? *(Acknowledge student answers)*

It would have been very easy for Selena to give up. Thankfully, when she felt overwhelmed with hopelessness, Selena knew what she needed to do; Selena asked for help. Selena's family and friends, her Hope Network, came to the rescue. Her family and friends supported her and helped her fight her hopelessness and fear. Her friend, Francia Raisa, even gave Selena one of her kidneys.

Once Selena had recovered from the surgery, she used her hope skills to fight her hope supervillains. Selena says that her secret to staying healthy is routine, diet, and medication. She also makes sure to spend time with the people in her Hope Network, and to practice her Stress Skills and Happiness Habits daily.

Selena decided that she should use her hope skills to help others. Selena is the youngest ambassador of the United Nations International Children's Emergency Fund (UNICEF), and has travelled around the world to help children in need. She has also shared her story in the hopes that it will inspire others to use their hope skills and ask for help when they face obstacles in their lives.

HOPEFUL MINDS LESSON THREE: Challenges to Hope

HOPE HERO SPOTLIGHT CNT'D

Every day, Selena uses her hope skills to keep moving forward and pursuing her goals. In an interview, Selena said: "It's always challenges which show you who you are and what you are capable of overcoming. I am proud of the person I am becoming."

Just like Magic Johnson, John Krasinski, and Selena Gomez, you have the ability to use your hope tools to achieve your dreams. There will be challenges, but you have the tools to overcome them. So, instead of fearing the unknown, look forward to it. Take good care of yourself and your emotions, wait to act until you are in your upstairs brain, and focus on your smart actions.

We believe in you. With hope, anything is possible!*

*This story was created from publicly available information. It does not suggest endorsement of Hopeful Minds, or any affiliation by known celebrity to our program. All information is for illustrative purposes for youth, to demonstrate skills used to create, maintain, and grow hope.

FINAL HOPE THOUGHTS
5 Minutes

Discuss the following questions with your class:

- How did Selena's Hope Network help her succeed?
- What are some skills Selena used to combat hopelessness to stay hopeful?
    - *Educators, you can talk about how she stayed focused on the present, didn't think she was a failure even when she failed, used her Hope Network, and stayed positive.*
- What do you all now think about hope? Is it important in your life? Are you going to practice?
- After these 3 lessons, what does hope now mean to you?
- Why is hope important?
- How do you plan to create a hopeful future?
- How do you think we can make hope skills cool and fun so that everyone wants to do them to increase hope in their lives?

Let us know if you or your students come up with new ways to make hope cool by emailing us at *activate@theshinehopecompany.com.*

HOPEFUL MINDS LESSON THREE: Challenges to Hope

HOPEFUL MINDS OVERVIEW CERTIFICATE OF COMPLETION

20 Minutes

Following your class discussion, have a ceremony for hope. Begin by having each student complete the Hope Emoji and Five Keys to Shine Hope Worksheets located at the end of this lesson. Encourage the students to think about all of the hope skills they've learned as they fill out their worksheets.

Consider displaying the completed Hope Emoji and Five Keys to Shine Hope Worksheets in your school hallways, or in local museums, art institutes, airports, businesses, or hospitals to help your students celebrate their hope journeys and share their messages of hope.

Once their worksheets are complete, give each student one of the Hope Certificates included at the end of this lesson. With their certificate, students will officially be "Hope Ambassadors," certified to both use hopeful practices in their own lives and teach them to others.

We are proud of the hope journey you and your class have taken, and we look forward to hearing more about the positive feelings, inspired actions, and SMART goals you are using in your lives and in your classroom.

HOPEFUL MINDS OVERVIEW CERTIFICATE OF COMPLETEION

Congratulations! iFred and Hopeful Minds are proud to present this Certificate of Completion to:

For completion of the Hopeful Minds Overview Hope Curriculum. We are proud of your commitment to use positive feelings, smart actions, Happiness Habits, and Stress Skills to inspire and foster hope in yourself and others. Thank you for your dedication and for becoming an official HOPEFUL MINDS AMBASSADOR.

Kathryn Goetzke
Kathryn Goetzke
Founder, iFred

_____
Teacher

☀ Hopeful Minds

HOPEFUL MINDS LESSON THREE: Challenges to Hope

ADDITIONAL ACTIVITIES FOR HOME OR VIRTUAL LEARNING

Consider using the following take-home activities to help students enhance their hope skills:

- Encourage students to use the Hope Journal pages at the end of their My Hopework Books to keep a journal of times they use their Five Keys to Shine Hope each day.
- John Krasinski, Magic Johnson, and Selena Gomez are three people who use their hope toolboxes to keep a hopeful mindset. However, they are not the only ones! Have students write their own Hope Hero Spotlight about a person in their lives who inspires them to hope. Before writing, encourage the students to answer the following questions:
    - How do you define a hero?
    - What do you think are some of the qualities in a hero?
    - How does this person use hope tools in their life?

    Their reports should introduce their hero, share why the person is their hero, and what hope skills they have used to succeed.
- Selena Gomez knows that giving hope is just as important as having hope. Help the students come up with ways that they can use their hope skills to help their parents, siblings, and people around them.
- Now that your students have expanded their hope toolboxes, they can be Hope Heroes as well! Have students write their own hope stories:
    - How are they using their hope tools to succeed?
    - How has hope helped them overcome obstacles?
    - What SMART goals do tbvhey have for the future?

MY HOPE EMOJI

HOPE IS:

HOPE LOOKS LIKE:

HOPE MEANS TO ME:

FIVE KEYS TO SHINE HOPE

MY HOPE HERO

HOW HOPEFUL ARE YOU?
Did you measure your hope? The lower your score, the more you want to practice these skills! Remember, hope is a muscle we need to build it (add it).

Check out here to get your hope score.

To write your hope hero journey, spend 20% of your time writing about their challenge, and 80% of the time sharing strategies for how they overcame it so others can learn from it. Here's how:

 1. Write your hope hero's name in the yellow line next to the box (feel free to use a nickname or anything else).

 2. Put your favorite photo of them on the yellow box, or an image of something that represents your hope hero.

 3. Write an introduction explaining the challenge they faced. Explain the two ingredients of hopelessness: despair (feelings) and helplessness (inability to act) they experienced.

 4. Share sadness, anger, fear, or other feelings, and choose 3 **Stress Skills** they used to navigate them (from the Shine infographic, or choose your own!).

 5. Share 3 **Happiness Habits** they used to get back to upstairs brain.

 6. Talk about 3 **Inspired Actions** they took, or share how your hope hero chunked down goals, the types of goals they've set, or if they had to regoal.

 7. Share who was in their **Nourishing Network**, and how it helped them navigate the challenge.

 8. Pick 3 challenges from the **'Eliminating Challenges'** on the infographic, and share how your hope hero eliminated them.

 9. Write the conclusion. What do you want the world to know? What do you wish someone had told you? What is the moral of the story?

If you're inspired, share this hope hero story so we can help activate these skills globally!

#Hope #ShineHope #MyHopeHero

> We all experience moments of hopelessness (emotional despair and motivational helplessness). The key is to use the Shine Hope skills to navigate your way from despair to positive feelings, and helplessness to inspired actions. Use the Shine Hope framework to build your muscle.

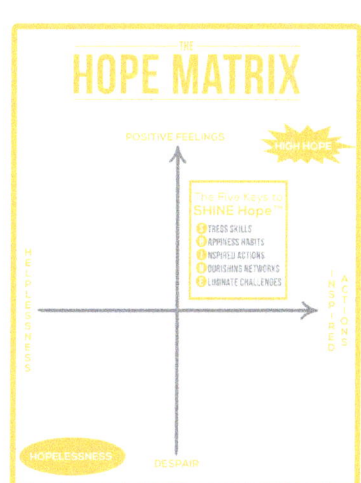

© 2024 The Shine Hope Company LLC.

MY HOPE HERO

☀️ ## Kathryn Goetzke

When Kathryn was 18 years old, a freshman at the University of Iowa, her dad died by suicide. It really changed her life. When she was in her early 20's, she then tried to take her own life, yet didn't tell another soul for 10 years. She knows a lot about hopelessness.

 To work on her recovery, she used a lot of Stress Skills. She talks about crying, going to therapy, learning to meditate, deep breathing, and listening to music. She traveled a lot, and took up hiking and exercise. She also took up boxing and spent a lot of time in nature.

 Kathryn was diligent about her Happiness Habits. She listened to her favorite band the Killers, went to concerts, focused on her nutrition and sleep, and started exercising. She pursued her passions, started a nonprofit iFred, and did a lot of volunteer work. She got serious about her purpose.

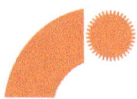 Kathryn also took a lot of Inspired Actions towards her goals. She chunked them down, got a degree and then an MBA. She couldn't talk to her dad anymore, so she found business mentors. Her brothers were always there to support her, and her mom was a source of strength and inspiration.

 Kathryn spent a lot of time with her Nourishing Networks. She spent time with people that were kind, compassionate, fun, and helped her heal. She had a therapist and got close to God. She had animals and spent a lot of time with wild horses in Nevada.

 She worked to Eliminate Challenges like her rumination and worry. She learned about sensory engagement, and even started a company to teach others. She worked to forgive herself and others. She focused on what she could control, which was her present and future, and did her best to let go of the rest. She put all her failures into teaching others.

Her use of the Shine Hope framework led her on a much healthier path. She has been sober almost 20 years, and had her nonprofit that same amount of time. She is a representative at the United Nations for the World Federation for Mental Health, and has shared her story around the world at places like the World Bank, Harvard, the United Nations, and more. She has created programming to teach hope to kids, published papers, and is now doing workplace programming, has a college, course, and is activating cities. She is on a mission to ensure all know how to hope, one person at a time. She is an inspiration, and someone that truly lives by example practicing all she teaches.

#Hope #ShineHope #MyHopeHero

MY HOPE HERO

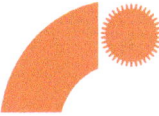

#Hope #ShineHope #MyHopeStory

MY SHINE HOPE STORY™

HOW HOPEFUL ARE YOU?

Did you measure your hope? The lower your score, the more you want to practice these skills! Remember, hope is a muscle we need to build it (add it).

Check out here to get your hope score.

To write your own shine hope story, spend 20% of your time writing about your challenge, and 80% of the time sharing strategies for how you overcame it so others can learn from you. Here's how:

 1. Write your name in the yellow line next to the box (feel free to use a nickname or anything else).

2. Put your favorite photo on the yellow box, or an image of something that represents you.

3. Write an introduction to your story explaining the challenge you faced. Explain the two ingredients of hopelessness: despair (feelings) and helplessness (inability to act) you experienced.

 4. Share sadness, anger, fear, or other feelings, and choose **3 Stress Skills** you used to naviate them (from the Shine infographic, or choose your own!).

 5. Share **3 Happiness Habits** you used to get back to your upstairs brain.

 6. Talk about **3 Inspired Actions** you took, or share how you chunked down goals, the types of goals you set, or if you had to regoal.

 7. Share who was in your **Nourishing Network**, and how they helped you navigate the challenge.

 8. Pick 3 challenges from the **'Eliminating Challenges'** on the infographic, and share how you eliminated them.

 9. Write your conclusion. What do you want the world to know? What do you wish someone had told you? What is the moral of the story?

If you're inspired, share your story so we can help activate these skills globally.

#Hope #ShineHope #MyShineHopeStory

We all experience moments of hopelessness (emotional despair and motivational helplessness). The key is to use the Shine Hope skills to navigate your way from despair to positive feelings, and helplessness to inspired actions. Use the Shine Hope framework to build your muscle.

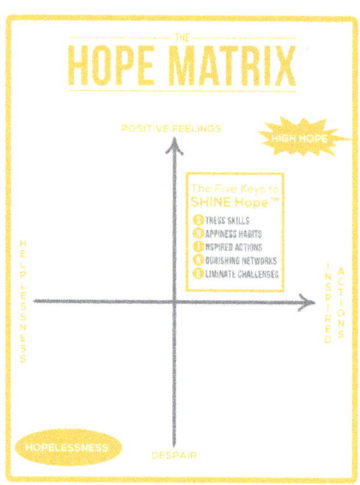

© 2024 The Shine Hope Company LLC.

MY SHINE HOPE STORY™

☀ ## Kathryn Goetzke

When I was 18 years old, a freshman at the University of Iowa, I called home and heard an unfamiliar, deep voice on the other line. It wasn't anyone I recognized, and he asked for my mom. My mom got on the phone to tell me my dad had taken his life. In that instance, my whole world crumbled. I felt a sadness so deep I thought I would never survive, and a helplessness so profound as I could not bring him back.

As hard as it was, I had to move forward. I started using Stress Skills to manage my pain. I cried when I was sad, started boxing to manage my anger, and learned how to start belly breathing to manage my fear. I listened to a lot of calming music when things got hard, and I started hiking all over the world. I also learned how to use sensory engagement to bring myself to the present moment.

Happiness Habits were critical. Sleep became an important part of my routine, and I started eating healthier foods. I cut alcohol out of my life. I replaced smoking with running, and made comedy clubs and laughter a part of my life. I listened to music, turned my sensory engagement passion into a purpose and started a company, and made volunteering a regular part of my life. I used dancing and live concerts (like my fave The Killers) as a form of release.

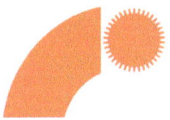

I also was very intentional about Inspired Actions. I had to chunk down my goals, leaving school and taking only one year at a time until I graduated. I had to regoal from having experiences with my dad to finding father-like figures to be in my life. I got closer to my brothers, their kids, and found mentors like Paul Carter and Dr. Belfer to guide me on my journey. My mom is my rock, my greatest source of strength and inspiration, keeping me moving forward towards my dreams.

Nourishing Networks were a constant. I stayed close to my friends and family, traveling, dancing, studying, and laughing. They were so compassionate, kind, generous, fun, and helped me heal. I forgave my dad for leaving, and forgave myself for not being there for him when he needed me. I got very close to God, understanding that I couldn't save my dad, and that in time this lesson would teach me how to help others.

It wasn't easy to Eliminate Challenges like rumination, internalizing failure, or worry. Yet I studied sensory engagement to be present when my mind started running. I deconstructed what led to my dad taking his life in a way that made it clear how to save myself and others. I knew that I couldn't control my dad, just like I can't control others. So I have focused on creating programming yet not being attached to if people want to learn it.

It's not been the easiest journey, and takes work. Yet by using the Shine Hope framework I have created a new life that is full of wonder, awe, happiness, adventure, and meaning. A different one than I expected, yet a beautiful one because I was able to dive in my pain, and learn the lessons necessary to teach others. And I use all my dad taught me in business to create a Shine Hope model for the world that ensures all know the what, why, and how of hope. And for that I know he is so very proud.

No matter what life brings, Keep Shining.

#Hope #ShineHope #MyHopeStory

© 2024 The Shine Hope Company LLC.

MY SHINE HOPE STORY™

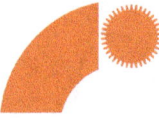

#Hope #ShineHope #MyHopeStory
© 2024 The Shine Hope Company LLC.

 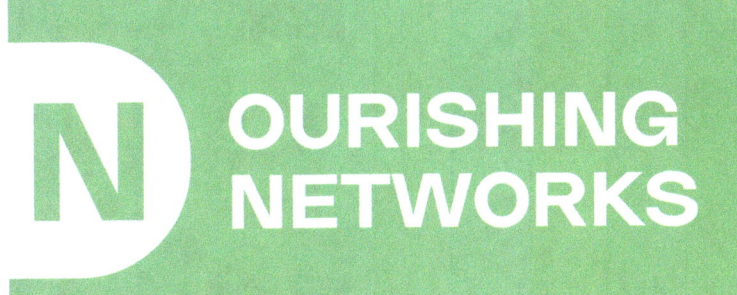

Nourishing Networks

Your Nourishing Networks, also known as your Hope Networks, are the people in your life that provide you with support, help you stay on track, encourage you to succeed, and who you do the same for in return. You are up to 95% more likely to achieve a goal if you write it down, and check in with someone regularly. So Nourishing Networks are critical support systems for moving you towards what you hope for in life.

Your Hope Networks should include:

- People who know and understand you.
- People who value your strengths.
- People who activate the SHINE framework.
- People whom you trust and can confide in.
- People who are available to support you.
- People you are willing to do the above for as well.

Enhancing Your Hope Networks

Enhance your Hope Networks using the 5:1 rule, vulnerability, praise, recognition, kindness, gratitude, empathy, compassion, collaboration, and strong communication, and be sure to have different networks for different areas of life.

Don't forget to include doctors, therapists, and/or other medical professionals in your Hope Networks.

© The Shine Hope Company, LLC

Challenges to Hope are negative habits of thought that quickly take you to hopelessness, that emotional despair and sense of helplessness. The thought patterns are often unconscious habits, so becoming aware of these patterns is critical. Once we know what they are and recognize them, it is important to counteract them so that we don't let them keep us from all we hope for in life.

Eliminating Challenges

Most of the Challenges to Hope take constant, repetitive actions to change and overcome. Thanks to the science of neuroplasticity, we know it is possible with practice and dedication. The key is to learn to identify what specific challenges happen most frequently and then proactively find ways to manage those challenges.

Limiting beliefs	Focusing on Uncontrollables	Mind Wandering
Automatic Negative Thoughts (ANTs)	Attaching to outcomes	Implicity Bias
All-or-nothing thinking	Internalizing failure	Negative Framing
Negative bias	Toxic Consumption	Perfectionism
Rumination & Worry	Nocebo Effect	Taking things personally

© The Shine Hope Company, LLC

HOPEFUL MINDS OVERVIEW
CERTIFICATE OF COMPLETION

Congratulations! iFred and Hopeful Minds are proud to present this

Certificate of Completion to:

For completion of the Hopeful Minds Overview Hope Curriculum. We are proud of your commitment to use positive feelings, smart actions, Happiness Habits, and Stress Skills to inspire and foster hope in yourself and others. Thank you for your dedication and for becoming an official HOPEFUL MINDS

AMBASSADOR.

Kathryn Goetzke
Kathryn Goetzke
Founder, iFred

_____
Teacher

Hopeful Minds

"I want people to feel hope and to know you will come out the other side stronger and a better version of yourself."

– Selena Gomez

ADDITIONAL ACTIVITY

Planting Sunflowers Growing Hope

ADDITIONAL ACTIVITY
PLANTING FLOWERS, GROWING HOPE

Hope is fueled by two main ingredients: positive feelings and inspired actions. While we aim for positive feelings, it is critical we teach kids not to run from negative ones, as these can be used to inform. Instead of dismissing negative feelings, we should encourage children to experience all of their feelings, learn how to express their negative ones in healthy ways, and then get themselves back to positive feelings before taking any action.

BACKGROUND INFORMATION FOR EDUCATORS

Sunflowers are an annual plant that are commonly bright yellow with a spiral center. There is great diversity in sunflowers, with a lot of varieties in sizes, colors, and shapes. The largest sunflower varieties can grow over 16 feet in height, while the smallest varieties barely reach 12 inches.

The sunflower is our representation of hope because, like hope, sunflowers bring positive feelings to all who see them, both men and women. Sunflowers are incredibly resilient; like hope, they can withstand almost anything nature throws at them. They grow in a variety of climates.

They also grow out of darkness, into the light. They are the most human-like flower, with a big bright face as a head, and petals like hair. They grow almost in a 'prayer position', with two leaves popping out like arms as they mature. Their faces follow the sunlight during the day.

You can also keep the sunflower of life going with sunflowers, by harvesting their seeds. You can replant these seeds in the next season, thus keeping hope alive. Hope is best when recycled and shared.

PLANT SUNFLOWER GARDENS TO SHINE HOPE

Gardening is a great time to practice the Shine Hope Framework, as we have a lot of challenges while planting a garden and we can go from hope to hopelessness pretty quickly. Yet that is a normal part of life, so gardening is an easy place to start practicing these skills.

Say you find some tough ground you need to dig into to plant, you may get frustrated and give up. It is a good time to practice a **Stress Skill** like a 90-second pause or deep breathing, to calm down your stress response. Then try again! You may also notice when others get frustrated and teach them how to use this skill to navigate from their downstairs brain back upstairs.

Eating the sunflower seeds (if ok with your doctor) might be a good way for you to practice your **Happiness Habits.** Sunflower seeds are nutritious, high in choline and selenium, great for brain function and memory. You might also get some exercise planting gardens, and spend time in nature, two other Happiness Habits and great ways to release endorphins.

Planting gardens remind us to take **Inspired Actions** by setting specific goals for the garden. If we want a garden, we need to set a SMART goal about how many flowers, when and where we want the garden, and how we are going to grow the flowers. It is best if we write down the plan, chunk it down into actionable steps, think about obstacles and multiple ways we might overcome them, and check in with someone regularly to ensure progress.

We can cultivate our **Nourishing Networks** by planting gardens with others. That way, if we have challenges while planting, we can face them together and be more creative about overcoming them. And if we don't live by the person we want to plant with, we can both decide to plant and check in regularly on the garden. It is also super fun to plan community gardens, or even fields of sunflowers, and all join together in learning and practicing skills to Shine Hope.

And finally, time to get serious about **Eliminating Challenges**. For example, if our sunflowers die and we fail for a season of planting, it is easy for us to think of ourselves as failures. Yet we aren't failures, our process failed. So deconstruct the process. Did we under or over water? Did we plant at the wrong time of year? Was something wrong with the soil? Did we overwater? It is time to investigate, and instead of ruminating about the sunflowers start figuring out what we can do better to try again next year.

Planting sunflowers is a way to spread the message of hope, as if you put up a Gardens of Hope sign with the website, people can then find the curriculum to learn more about the programs for 'how' to hope. Our program is available around the world, and gardens are a great way to share the message that Hope is Teachable.

Find out more at www.hopefulcities.org   @theshinehopecompany

HOPEFUL MINDS OVERVIEW: Additional Activity

Additional Resources for Educators

- Burpee: All About Sunflowers
- How to Grow Sunflowers
- The Farmer's Almanac Guide to Growing Sunflowers

HOPEFUL MINDS OVERVIEW: Additional Activity

ACTIVITY OVERVIEW
Total Instruction Time: 30 Minutes

FORMAT

Discussion
Sunflower Planting Activity

ACTIVITY OBJECTIVES

Understand How Hope Helps Us Grow
Learn How to Spread Hope by Leading by Example

PRINT-OUTS FOR EDUCATORS
Hopeful Minds Sign for Your Garden (Optional)

PRINT-OUTS FOR STUDENTS
None

ACTIVITY OUTLINE

10 Min   Why Sunflowers

20 Min   Planting Sunflower Seeds

ACTIVITY PREPARATION

Prior to the lesson, prepare the following materials:

- Purchase sunflower seeds and tools for planting, including shovel and watering can
- Locate and demarcate location for sunflowers

HOPEFUL MINDS OVERVIEW: Additional Activity

WHY SUNFLOWERS?
10 Minutes

Read the following to your students:

Helping others and giving back is a very important part of staying hopeful. It feels good to support other people, reminds us that we are not alone, and allows us to feel compassion and empathy.

We are going to practice giving back today by planting sunflowers that can be enjoyed by next year's students.

Now, let's talk about why we have chosen sunflowers to plant.

We were very deliberate in our choosing of the sunflowers. It all began from a study by the Emotional Impact of Flowers Study conducted by Jeannette M. Haviland-Jones, Ph.D., Professor of Psychology, Project Director, Human Development Lab at Rutgers. According to her research, regardless of age, flowers have an immediate impact on happiness. Recent studies have suggested flowers help reduce stress, and often increase serotonin and dopamine.

- The symbolism of the sunflower holds profound meaning. A sunflower seed begins its journey in darkness, mirroring our most hopeless states. It represents our potential for growth and improvement amid despair. Just as a seed cannot flourish alone, we, too, rely on our Hope Network to nurture our hope.

- The growth of a sunflower echoes our journey toward hope. It stretches roots deep into the ground, akin to our efforts to break free from despair using Stress Skills—meditation, deep breathing, and mindful pauses.

- As the sunflower emerges into the sunlight, it unfurls leaves to gather sunshine, needing water, nourishment, and care to flourish. Similarly, we cultivate positive feelings through Happiness Habits—long-term, healthy practices fostering more and more hope.

WHY SUNFLOWERS? CNT'D

- Obstacles pepper the sunflower's path; rocky soil and inadequate resources. Likewise, we face challenges. However, equipped with Stress Skills, Happiness Habits, Inspired Actions, Nourishing Networks, and skills to Eliminate Challenges, we navigate and conquer these hurdles.

- The sunflower's purpose transcends its growth; it provides sustenance and joy. Similarly, we share hope with those around us, becoming beacons of optimism and joy.

- Our choice of the sunflower and its vibrant yellow hue isn't arbitrary. It symbolizes our commitment to shine a positive light on hope, eradicating mental health stigma through proactive measures in prevention, research, and education. Yellow is the color of happiness and hope.

- Gardening is also very healthy for the mood, so we encourage community gardens. Eating sunflower seeds can be healthy for the brain, as they are rich in vital nutrients. It is also one of the only flowers that can be planted anywhere in the world, and we believe the 'how' to hope must be planted everywhere as well.

- It is also a method for nonprofits to raise funds for hope. You can sell the seeds, have gardens sponsored, sell products in retail, or create art for auctions. The ideas are endless!

So, in this endeavor, the sunflower becomes more than a symbol—it becomes the embodiment of hope, illuminating pathways toward a brighter future for cities and individuals alike.

HOPEFUL MINDS OVERVIEW: Additional Activity

PLANTING SUNFLOWERS ACTIVITY
20 Minutes

By planting sunflowers, we are creating a physical representation of how spreading hope can improve both our lives and the lives of those around us. It is also a way to spread the message of hope, as if you put up a Gardens of Hope sign with the website, people can then find the curriculum to learn more about it themselves. Our program is available around the world, and gardens are a great way to share the message.

To plant your sunflowers from seeds:

- Sunflowers should be planted between May and July (depending on where you live, you will need to look at your specific climate) once the last frost has melted.
- Space seeds 12 to 48 inches apart, depending on the size of your sunflower variety.
- Seeds should be placed 1 to 2 inches deep in clayey soils and 2+ inches deep in
- sandy soils.
- A small amount of fertilizer mixed in during planting will encourage root growth.
- While the sunflowers are growing, water around the root zone (3 to 4 inches from the plant) once a day.
- Once the plants are established, water less frequently but more deeply.

Most sunflower varieties will mature in 80 to 120 days. Once sunflowers develop seeds, harvest seeds with students to save for planting next season. As you can see, lots of fun ways to practice how to Shine Hope when we garden. Share with us how it went for you, pictures from your sunflowers, ways you practiced your skills, and help us all get better.

Tag us @theshinehopecompany @ifredorg #ShineHope #GardensForHope #Hope

Hopeful Minds

Plant Seeds. Shine Light. Grow Hope.

We are hopeful for:

#hopefulminds #teachhope

www.hopefulminds.org

@ifred.org

SUNFLOWERS... Fascinating Facts

The tallest sunflower was grown in the Netherlands by M. Heijmf in 1986 and was 25' 5.5" tall.

The sunflower plant reaches heights of 3 to 18 feet within just 90 to 100 days and produces a seed head with up to 2,000 seeds arranged in a spiral pattern.

The sunflower has heliotropic behaviors, meaning always turns their face toward the sun, which is a great metaphor for looking toward the future with hope.

I AM MANY
The yellow petals are actually the the protective leaves that cover the head while it is growing. That brown center is made up of hundreds of individually growing flowers, where a sunflower seed will emerge.

I LIKE EVERYBODY
Within the last few years, a new form of low-pollen sunflower has been created to help reduce the risk of asthma for pollen sufferers.

Sunflowers are resilient and able to grow in harsh environments, such as dry and rocky soil. They grow out of the darkness and into the light, moving through challenging times with not much light. Yet they make it. This ability to thrive in tough conditions is a powerful symbol of hope and perseverance.

I HAVE POTENTIAL
Sunflower oil can be made into plastics, and research has also revealed that it the potential to create fuel for automobiles and other machinery.

I AM ANCIENT!
The sunflower was domesticated from wild sunflowers around 1000 B.C. by Native Americans. It was ground into flours for making breads and soups, while sunflower oil softened leather, salved wounds, and conditioned hair.

I HELP THE ENVIRONMENT
An emerging technology called rhizofiltration, hydroponically grown sunflowers are grown floating over water. Their extensive root systems reach deep into sources of polluted water and extract large amounts of toxic metals, including uranium. The roots were able to extract 95% of the radioactivity in the water left behind by the accident at Chernobyl.

I BRING THE WORLD TOGETHER
Brought to the U.S. in 1996 from Russia, one of the largest areas of sunflower growth in the world, is in the former Soviet Union, which is second only to Argentina. The simple prairie sunflower, native to North America, is now one of the worlds leading oil seed crops behind soy beans.

Sunflowers are often used to symbolize new beginnings, growth, and renewal. This makes them a perfect symbol of hope, as they represent the idea of starting fresh and growing toward a brighter future.

> "Keep your face to the sunshine and you cannot see the shadow. It's what sunflowers do."
> — Helen Keller

The Bonsai technique was used to make the shortest mature sunflower record. The sunflower was just over 2" tall.

I AM ROYAL — In Peru, the Aztecs worshipped sunflowers. They did so by placing sunflower images made of gold in their temples and crowning princesses in the bright yellow flowers.

Sunflowers are a bright yellow, and research suggests people who were surrounded by brighter and more vibrant colors reported higher levels of positive emotions, such as happiness and excitement.

Follow us: @ifredorg

iFred, a 501(c)3 organization, is working to teach hope, shine a positive light on mental health, and end the stigma around mental illness. iFred has started a number of programs to activate hope around the world, including Hopeful Minds®, Hopeful Cities®, and International Day of Hope. Learn more at www.ifred.org.

HOPEFUL MINDS OVERVIEW
HOPEWORK BOOK

Name: _____

Language: English

These materials are designed to assist you in learning about hope. They should not be used for medical advice, counseling, or other health-related services. iFred, The Shine Hope Company and Kathryn Goetzke do not endorse or provide any medical advice, diagnosis, or treatment. The information provided herein should not be used for the diagnosis or treatment of any medical condition and cannot be substituted for the advice of physicians, licensed professionals, or therapists who are familiar with your specific situation. Consult a licensed medical professional, or call 911, if you are in need of immediate assistance.

© 2020, Kathryn Goetzke.

All rights reserved. No part of this book may be reproduced, shared or distributed without the written permission of the publisher.

For more information, please contact kathryngoetzke@theshinehopecompany.com.

We designed The Hopework book to be used alongside the Hopeful Minds Overview Curriculum, free for download at www.hopefulminds.org. We encourage you to use this program at home, in school, place of worship, during after-school programs, with police teaching youth programs, or anywhere where there are groups of people eager to activate hope.

No special training is required to use our Hopework book, as it was tailored for all age groups. While the book was written for anyone who can read English, parents, caregivers, or teachers may need to assist young children who are still learning to read.

Our workbook can be used with any population. We believe hope is a skill anyone and everyone should develop, as research has found hope to be impactful in many areas of life. We ALL need to know how to proactively manage hopelessness and have skills to activate hope.

The Overview is an introduction into the 'what, why, and how' of hope. We encourage you to use our Hopeful Minds Deep Dive upon completion of the Hopework book, and check out our other resources available including a Parent's Guide.

While you work through the materials, we ask that you share the images from the workbook on social media, to help us learn and inspire others on the 'how' to hope. **Tag @ifredorg @theshinehopecompany and use hashtags #HopefulMinds #Hope #ShineHope #FiveKeysToShineHope #GrowHope as you post.** For our younger users, make sure to get parent permission prior to posting anything on social media. Thank you for choosing hope not only for yourself, but for those who share and teach along the way. Together, we can improve our collective future hope is key to creating all we want.

HOPE SCALES

What you cannot measure, you cannot improve. It is therefore important to measure your hope levels to monitor your progress and check in on yourself. While there are many scales for hope, we use the Children and Adult Snyder Hope Scales to measure hope, as they have been used in many studies on hope. By taking the Snyder Hope Scale regularly, you can begin to see the link between hope and outcomes in every area of your life.

Hope is a journey; as you move forward, your hope levels will rise and fall. That is okay. If you practice your hope skills regularly, no matter how hopeless life seems in the low moments, you will always have a way back to hope.

We ask that you measure your hope, and encourage all those in your community to measure hope, so we can start tracking hopefulness in individuals around the world. As you work through the Hopeful Minds curriculum, consider administering the hope scale multiple times so the students can keep track of their hope level changes.

Use the link provided to take the Snyder Hope Scale Assessment or scan the QR code below. *(with permission of legal guardian)*:

www.theshinehopecompany.com/measure-your-hope/

Children's Hope Scale

Adult Hope Scale

My current Snyder Hope Scale Score:

How do you feel about your score?

How hopeful have you been in your life?

How has your hope impacted your ability to achieve goals?

In what areas of your life do you feel like you could be more hopeful?

This course teaches you the hope skills you can use to create, maintain, and grow hope. There will be times throughout your life when you or someone you love experiences hopelessness. It is at these times, when your hope score is at its lowest, that it is most important to practice skills to activate hope.

The goal of this course is to learn the "how-to" of hope so that you can both create a model for your own life and share the power of hope with others.

Who in your life could benefit from higher hope?

What organizations or businesses in your community could benefit from learning about hope?

STRENGTHS FINDER

Understanding your strengths is another important tool for creating and maintaining hope. Focusing on your strengths can help you manage your stress response, cultivate positive thoughts, and focus on the future. Additionally, understanding strengths allows one to capitalize on their strengths while moving toward inspired actions, a necessary element in hope. Use this tool with yourself, and others. We want to focus on the children's strengths as opposed to what they are doing wrong because recognizing strengths in children can help them build confidence and support their life-long pursuit of hope. As you continue through this workbook, you will repeatedly be asked to reflect on your strengths. It is a positive way to create a more hopeful future.

You can check out your strengths here *(with permission of legal guardian)*:

www.hopefulmindsets.pro.viasurvey.org

Write down the top five strengths from your results:

1. _____
2. _____
3. _____
4. _____
5. _____

Which of these strengths do you think is most tied to your ability to grow and maintain hope?

_____
_____

Are you activating your strengths regularly? How so?

_____
_____

How can you better utilize your strengths at home? At work?

_____
_____

LESSON 1 WORKSHEETS

THE WHAT AND WHY OF HOPE

Please tag us on social media @ifredorg @theshinehopecompany to share your completed work and use the hashtags: #HopefulMinds #Hope #ShineHope #FiveKeysToShineHope #GrowHope #WhatAndWhyOfHope

THE HOPE MATRIX

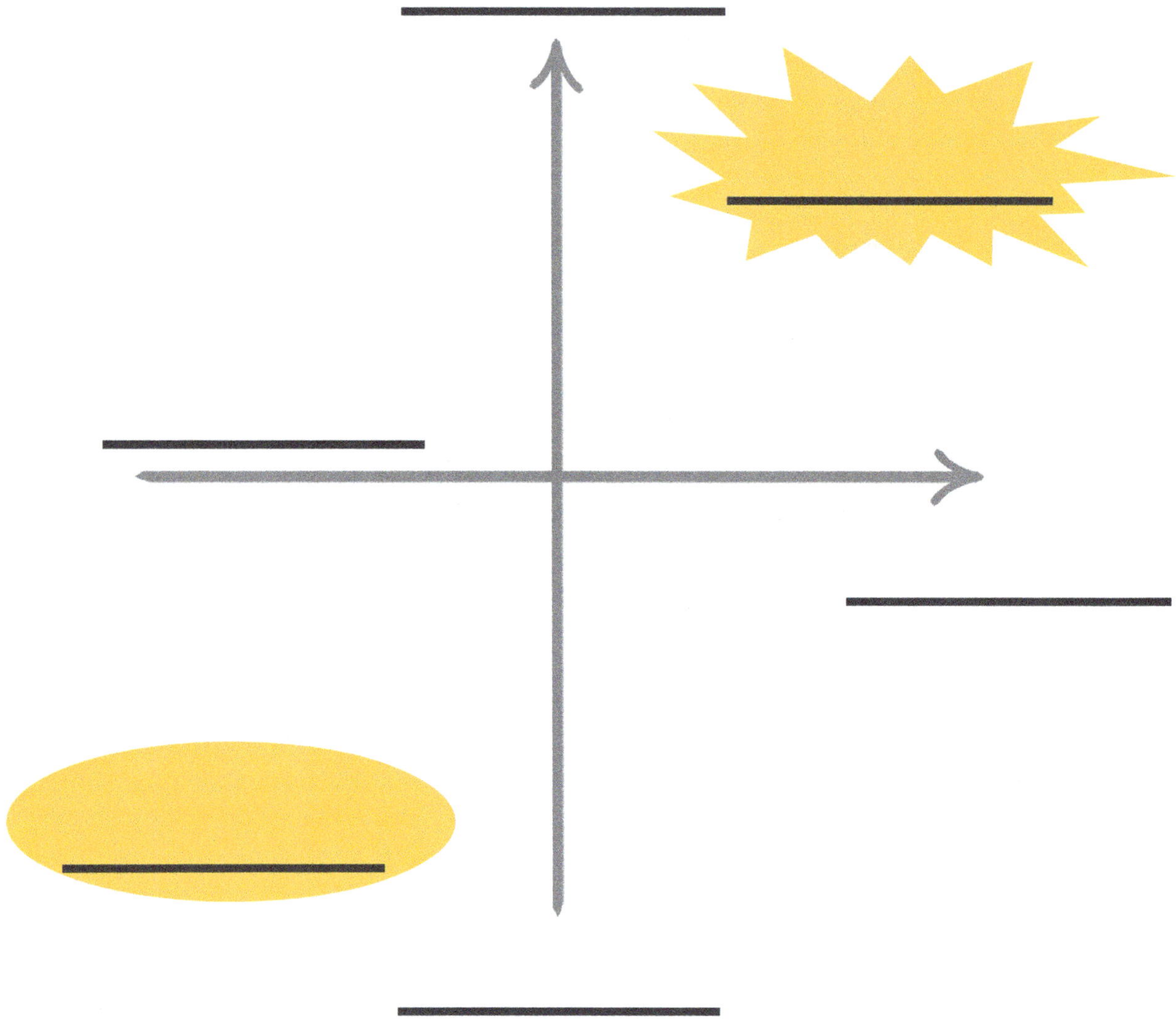

Directions: Fill in the blanks above with the following words: Hope, Hopelessness, Despair, Helplessness, Positive Feelings, Inspired Actions.

Five Keys to Shine Hope

Directions: Write the Five Keys to Shine Hope below and color the letters.

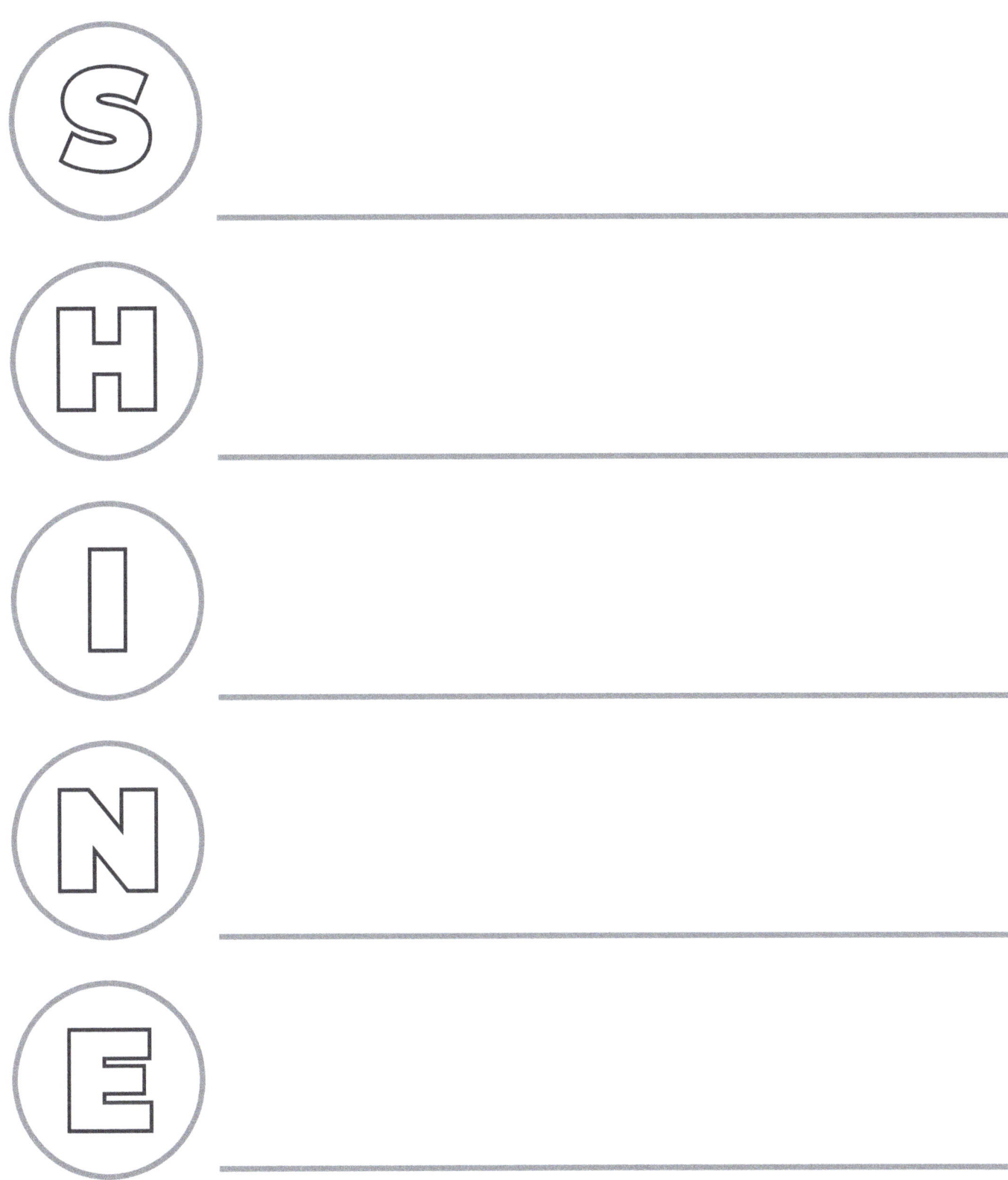

107

STOP. *BREATHE.* RELAX.

Directions: Circle your top four favorite stress skills from the list below. If there are additional stress skills you use that are not on the list, use the space below the add them.

Stress Skills

- 90 Second Pause
- Deep Belly Breathing
- Napping
- Calming Music
- Reaffirming beliefs
- Visualization
- Sensory Engagement
- Punching a Pillow
- Crying
- Prayer
- Walk in Nature
- Meditation
- Yoga
- Decluttering
- Focus on Strengths
- Journaling
- Exercise
- Gardening
- Time Near Water and Nature

MY FAVORITE STRESS SKILLS

-
-
-
-
-
-
-
-

HAPPINESS HABITS

Directions: Circle your top four favorite happiness habits from the list below. If there are additional happiness habits you use that are not on the list, use the space below the add them.

- Utilizing strengths
- Pursuing passion
- Activating purpose
- Smiling
- Exercising
- Playing or Listening to Music
- Spending time in Nature
- Showing Gratitude and Kindness
- Playing Games
- Volunteering
- Time with Family and Friends
- Experiencing Wonder & Awe
- Practicing Faith
- Sleeping
- Nutrition
- Dancing and Singing
- Donating
- Giving a hug
- Setting Goals
- Practicing Affirmations

My favorite happiness habits:

-
-
-
-
-
-
-

MY HOPE SUNFLOWER

Directions: Start by filling in the sunflower's center with your definition of hope. Then, fill in the top part of the sunflower with three happiness habits that will help you remain in the upstairs brain. Finally, fill in the bottom part of the sunflower with three stress skills you can use to help when you find yourself in the downstairs brain.

Keep your face to the sunshine and you cannot see the shadow. It's what sunflowers do." -Helen Keller

LESSON 2 WORKSHEETS

EMOTIONS AND SMART ACTIONS

Please tag us on social media @ifredorg @theshinehopecompany to share your completed work and use the hashtags: #HopefulMinds #Hope #ShineHope #FiveKeysToShineHope #GrowHope #WhatAndWhyOfHope

FEELINGS WORKSHEET

Directions: Fill in each column based on the emotions on the left.

I. IDENTIFYING FEELINGS

Emotion	What does it look like?	Where do I feel it?	Where is it my brain? (circle one)
HAPPY	○		▲ UPSTAIRS ▼ DOWNSTAIRS
ANGRY	○		▲ UPSTAIRS ▼ DOWNSTAIRS
SAD	○		▲ UPSTAIRS ▼ DOWNSTAIRS
SCARED	○		▲ UPSTAIRS ▼ DOWNSTAIRS

II. MY HOPE EMOTICON

Directions: Using the space at the side, draw an emoticon for hope.

#HopefulMinds #Hope #ShineHope #FiveKeysToShineHope #GrowHope #MyFeelingsMatter

MY BRAIN

I. Directions: Fill in the blanks with the emotions of the emoticon facial expressions that match using *fear, anger, sadness, relaxed, happy,* and *excited*.

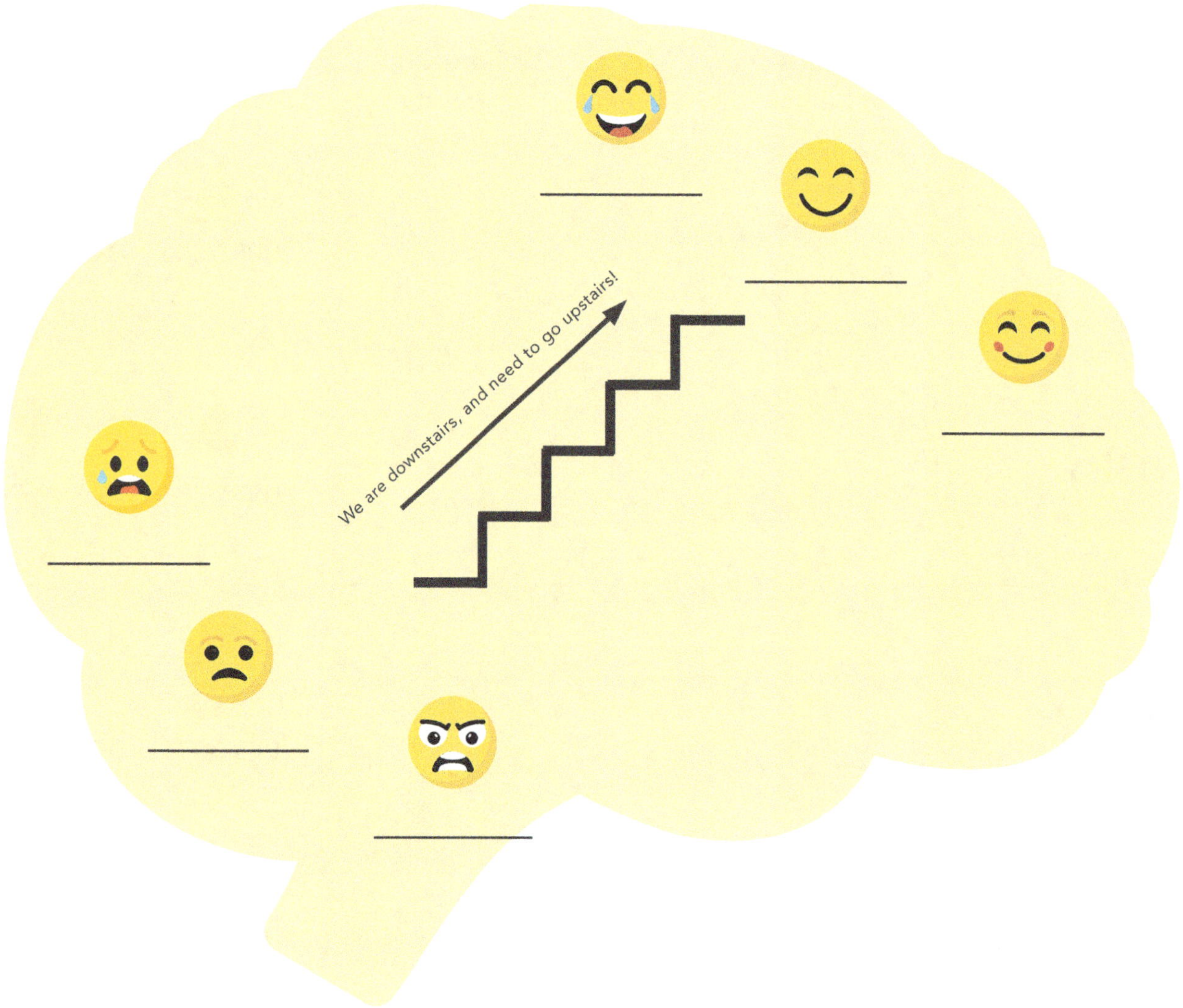

II. Directions: Draw how your body feels when you are in your upstairs and downstairs brain.

UPSTAIRS   DOWNSTAIRS

S.M.A.R.T. GOALS

Specific
Be specific about your goal. Think about these questions when creating your goal: What needs to be accomplished? Who is responsible for it? What steps will you take to achieve it?

Measurable
Can you measure your progress? If this goal will take a long time to achieve, set shorter term goals to reach along the way.

Achievable
Are you inspired and motivated to reach your goal? Do you have the tools or skills you need? If not, do you know how you can get them?

Relevant
Does your goal make sense? Does it go along with what you are trying to achieve in the bigger picture?

Time-bound
Is your timing realistic? Can you achieve your goal in the time period set? Think about what you may want to achieve at the halfway point.

INSPIRED ACTIONS

Directions: Write or draw answers to each of the prompts below.

My classroom goal this week is:

I will help myself reach my goal by:

Things that could keep me from reaching my goal:

Ways I will overcome those obstacles:

LESSON 3 WORKSHEETS

CHALLENGES TO HOPE

Please tag us on social media @ifredorg @theshinehopecompany to share your completed work and use the hashtags: #HopefulMinds #Hope #ShineHope #FiveKeysToShineHope #GrowHope #WhatAndWhyOfHope

NOURISHING NETWORK

Directions: Write or draw answers to each of the prompts below.

Friends and family I can count on and confide in:

People I turn to for Stress Skills:

People I practice Happiness Habits with:

Things I can connect to:
ex. Spiritual Advisor, Peer Support, Animals, Nature, etc.

Teachers, doctors, and experts I go to for support:

Community Resources I can utilize:

Where can I go to in times of crisis? *ex. If you can't list anyone, you can check out our list of resources for how to get connected. Visit https://hopefulcities.org/get-support/*

One person I can always count on even if we aren't close:

HOPE SUPERVILLAINS

Directions: Draw the supervillains and monsters listed in the boxes below. Write answers to the orange prompts.

Draw your HOPE Superhero

OUR HOPE HERO DEFEATS OUR HOPE VILLAINS!

I Worry About: _____

My Worry Monster:

I Ruminate On: _____

My Rumination Monster:

I Failed At: _____

My Failure Monster:

I Feel Hopelessness Because: _____

My Hopelessness Monster:

#HopefulMinds #Hope #ShineHope #FiveKeysToShineHope #GrowHope #HopeSupervillains

CONTROL THE CONTROLLABLES

Directions: List or draw the things you CAN control in the space inside the sunflower. List or draw the things you CAN'T control in the space around the sunflower.

THINGS THAT I CAN CONTROL

THINGS THAT I CANNOT CONTROL

#HopefulMinds #Hope #ShineHope #FiveKeysToShineHope #GrowHope #HopeSupervillains

HOPE WORKSHEET

Directions: Fill in each box with a drawing or 1-3 sentences of writing.

Draw something you are hopeful for:

Write about what you are hopeful for:

Hope is important because:

#HopefulMinds #Hope #ShineHope #FiveKeysToShineHope #GrowHope #ImHopefulFor

MY HOPE HERO

HOW HOPEFUL ARE YOU?
Did you measure your hope? The lower your score, the more you want to practice these skills! Remember, hope is a muscle we need to build it (add it).

Check out here to get your hope score.

To write your hope hero journey, spend 20% of your time writing about their challenge, and 80% of the time sharing strategies for how they overcame it so others can learn from it. Here's how:

 1. Write your hope hero's name in the yellow line next to the box (feel free to use a nickname or anything else).

 2. Put your favorite photo of them on the yellow box, or an image of something that represents your hope hero.

 3. Write an introduction explaining the challenge they faced. Explain the two ingredients of hopelessness: despair (feelings) and helplessness (inability to act) they experienced.

 4. Share sadness, anger, fear, or other feelings, and choose 3 **Stress Skills** they used to navigate them (from the Shine infographic, or choose your own!).

 5. Share 3 **Happiness Habits** they used to get back to upstairs brain.

 6. Talk about 3 **Inspired Actions** they took, or share how your hope hero chunked down goals, the types of goals they've set, or if they had to regoal.

 7. Share who was in their **Nourishing Network**, and how it helped them navigate the challenge.

 8. Pick 3 challenges from the **'Eliminating Challenges'** on the infographic, and share how your hope hero eliminated them.

 9. Write the conclusion. What do you want the world to know? What do you wish someone had told you? What is the moral of the story?

If you're inspired, share this hope hero story so we can help activate these skills globally!

#Hope #ShineHope #MyHopeHero

> We all experience moments of hopelessness (emotional despair and motivational helplessness). The key is to use the Shine Hope skills to navigate your way from despair to positive feelings, and helplessness to inspired actions. Use the Shine Hope framework to build your muscle.

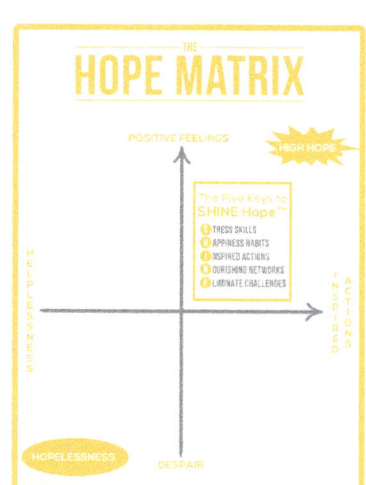

© 2024 The Shine Hope Company LLC.

MY HOPE HERO

☀ ## Kathryn Goetzke

When Kathryn was 18 years old, a freshman at the University of Iowa, her dad died by suicide. It really changed her life. When she was in her early 20's, she then tried to take her own life, yet didn't tell another soul for 10 years. She knows a lot about hopelessness.

To work on her recovery, she used a lot of Stress Skills. She talks about crying, going to therapy, learning to meditate, deep breathing, and listening to music. She traveled a lot, and took up hiking and exercise. She also took up boxing and spent a lot of time in nature.

Kathryn was diligent about her Happiness Habits. She listened to her favorite band the Killers, went to concerts, focused on her nutrition and sleep, and started exercising. She pursued her passions, started a nonprofit iFred, and did a lot of volunteer work. She got serious about her purpose.

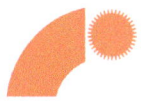
Kathryn also took a lot of Inspired Actions towards her goals. She chunked them down, got a degree and then an MBA. She couldn't talk to her dad anymore, so she found business mentors. Her brothers were always there to support her, and her mom was a source of strength and inspiration.

Kathryn spent a lot of time with her Nourishing Networks. She spent time with people that were kind, compassionate, fun, and helped her heal. She had a therapist and got close to God. She had animals and spent a lot of time with wild horses in Nevada.

She worked to Eliminate Challenges like her rumination and worry. She learned about sensory engagement, and even started a company to teach others. She worked to forgive herself and others. She focused on what she could control, which was her present and future, and did her best to let go of the rest. She put all her failures into teaching others.

Her use of the Shine Hope framework led her on a much healthier path. She has been sober almost 20 years, and had her nonprofit that same amount of time. She is a representative at the United Nations for the World Federation for Mental Health, and has shared her story around the world at places like the World Bank, Harvard, the United Nations, and more. She has created programming to teach hope to kids, published papers, and is now doing workplace programming, has a college, course, and is activating cities. She is on a mission to ensure all know how to hope, one person at a time. She is an inspiration, and someone that truly lives by example practicing all she teaches.

#Hope #ShineHope #MyHopeHero

MY HOPE HERO

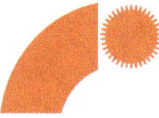

#Hope #ShineHope #MyHopeStory

MY SHINE HOPE STORY™

HOW HOPEFUL ARE YOU?
Did you measure your hope? The lower your score, the more you want to practice these skills! Remember, hope is a muscle we need to build it (add it).

Check out here to get your hope score.

To write your own shine hope story, spend 20% of your time writing about your challenge, and 80% of the time sharing strategies for how you overcame it so others can learn from you. Here's how:

 1. Write your name in the yellow line next to the box (feel free to use a nickname or anything else).

2. Put your favorite photo on the yellow box, or an image of something that represents you.

3. Write an introduction to your story explaining the challenge you faced. Explain the two ingredients of hopelessness: despair (feelings) and helplessness (inability to act) you experienced.

 4. Share sadness, anger, fear, or other feelings, and choose **3 Stress Skills** you used to naviate them (from the Shine infographic, or choose your own!).

 5. Share **3 Happiness Habits** you used to get back to your upstairs brain.

 6. Talk about **3 Inspired Actions** you took, or share how you chunked down goals, the types of goals you set, or if you had to regoal.

 7. Share who was in your **Nourishing Network**, and how they helped you navigate the challenge.

 8. Pick 3 challenges from the **'Eliminating Challenges'** on the infographic, and share how you eliminated them.

9. Write your conclusion. What do you want the world to know? What do you wish someone had told you? What is the moral of the story?

If you're inspired, share your story so we can help activate these skills globally.

#Hope #ShineHope #MyShineHopeStory

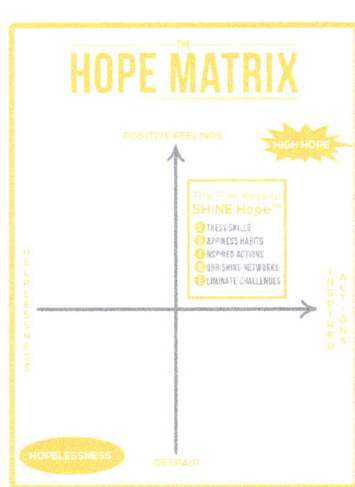

> We all experience moments of hopelessness (emotional despair and motivational helplessness). The key is to use the Shine Hope skills to navigate your way from despair to positive feelings, and helplessness to inspired actions. Use the Shine Hope framework to build your muscle.

© 2024 The Shine Hope Company LLC.

MY SHINE HOPE STORY™

☀ Kathryn Goetzke

When I was 18 years old, a freshman at the University of Iowa, I called home and heard an unfamiliar, deep voice on the other line. It wasn't anyone I recognized, and he asked for my mom. My mom got on the phone to tell me my dad had taken his life. In that instance, my whole world crumbled. I felt a sadness so deep I thought I would never survive, and a helplessness so profound as I could not bring him back.

As hard as it was, I had to move forward. I started using Stress Skills to manage my pain. I cried when I was sad, started boxing to manage my anger, and learned how to start belly breathing to manage my fear. I listened to a lot of calming music when things got hard, and I started hiking all over the world. I also learned how to use sensory engagement to bring myself to the present moment.

Happiness Habits were critical. Sleep became an important part of my routine, and I started eating healthier foods. I cut alcohol out of my life. I replaced smoking with running, and made comedy clubs and laughter a part of my life. I listened to music, turned my sensory engagement passion into a purpose and started a company, and made volunteering a regular part of my life. I used dancing and live concerts (like my fave The Killers) as a form of release.

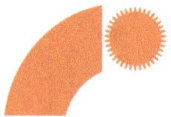

I also was very intentional about Inspired Actions. I had to chunk down my goals, leaving school and taking only one year at a time until I graduated. I had to regoal from having experiences with my dad to finding father-like figures to be in my life. I got closer to my brothers, their kids, and found mentors like Paul Carter and Dr. Belfer to guide me on my journey. My mom is my rock, my greatest source of strength and inspiration, keeping me moving forward towards my dreams.

Nourishing Networks were a constant. I stayed close to my friends and family, traveling, dancing, studying, and laughing. They were so compassionate, kind, generous, fun, and helped me heal. I forgave my dad for leaving, and forgave myself for not being there for him when he needed me. I got very close to God, understanding that I couldn't save my dad, and that in time this lesson would teach me how to help others.

It wasn't easy to Eliminate Challenges like rumination, internalizing failure, or worry. Yet I studied sensory engagement to be present when my mind started running. I deconstructed what led to my dad taking his life in a way that made it clear how to save myself and others. I knew that I couldn't control my dad, just like I can't control others. So I have focused on creating programming yet not being attached to if people want to learn it.

It's not been the easiest journey, and takes work. Yet by using the Shine Hope framework I have created a new life that is full of wonder, awe, happiness, adventure, and meaning. A different one than I expected, yet a beautiful one because I was able to dive in my pain, and learn the lessons necessary to teach others. And I use all my dad taught me in business to create a Shine Hope model for the world that ensures all know the what, why, and how of hope. And for that I know he is so very proud.

No matter what life brings, Keep Shining.

#Hope #ShineHope #MyHopeStory

© 2024 The Shine Hope Company LLC.

MY SHINE HOPE STORY™

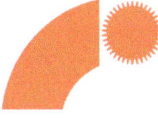

#Hope #ShineHope #MyHopeStory

© 2024 The Shine Hope Company LLC.

MY HOPE JOURNAL

1. How are you using your hope tools to succeed? Think about the SHINE acronym and how you've used it.

2. How has hope helped you overcome obstacles?

3. What SMART goals do you have for the future?

4. What can you control about the school year? What can't you control? How can you make the most of what they can control? How can you release emotions from what they can't control? How can you be creative about their experience this semester or year?

5. How do you define a hero? What do you think are some of the qualities in a hero? How does this person use hope tools in their life?

Please tag us on social media @ifredorg @theshinehopecompany to share your completed work and use the hashtags: #HopefulMinds #Hope #ShineHope #FiveKeysToShineHope #GrowHope #WhatAndWhyOfHope

MY HOPE JOURNAL

WHAT FUELS MY HOPE?

Hopeful Minds

Spread Hope. Tag us on social media @ifredorg @theshinehopecompany and use hashtags #HopefulMinds #Hope #ShineHope #FiveKeysToShineHope #GrowHope #Hopefuel

WHAT AM I HOPEFUL FOR?

Hopeful Minds

Spread Hope. Tag us on social media @ifredorg @theshinehopecompany and use hashtags #HopefulMinds #Hope #ShineHope #FiveKeysToShineHope #GrowHope #ImHopefulFor

Additional Resources for Educators

LESSON 1 RESOURCES

- Explaining the Brain to Children and Adolescents (https://vimeo.com/109042767)
- Heart Rate Variability: A New Way to Track Well-Being (https://www.health.harvard.edu/blog/heart-rate-variability-new-way-track-well-2017112212789)
- Gain Hope: A Place for Hope in the Age of Anxiety (http://www.gainhope.com/hope/default.cfm)
- Fight, Flight, Freeze Responses (https://trauma-recovery.ca/impact-effects-of-trauma/fight-flight-freeze-responses/)
- John Krasinski Biography (https://www.biography.com/actor/john-krasinski)
- Some Good News (https://www.youtube.com/channel/UCOe_y6KKvS3Pdlfb9q9pGug)

LESSON 2 RESOURCES

- SMART Goals: How to Make Your Goals Achievable (https://www.mindtools.com/pages/article/smart-goals.htm)
- The 90 Second Rule You Can't Afford to Ignore (https://onebodyinc.com/the-90-second-rule-you-cant-afford-to-ignore/)
- The Neuroanatomical Transformation of the Teenage Brain: Jill Bolte Taylor (https://www.youtube.com/watch?v=PzT_SBl31-s)
- Experiencing and Expressing Emotion (https://counselingcenter.illinois.edu/brochures/experiencing-and-expressing-emotion)
- Achieving Your Goals: An Evidence-Based Approach (https://www.canr.msu.edu/news/achieving_your_goals_an_evidence_based_approach)
- Zimbabwe Friendship Bench (https://www.friendshipbenchzimbabwe.org/)
- Voices Around the World (https://voicesaround.com/)
- Magic Johnson Biography (https://www.biography.com/athlete/magic-johnson)

LESSON 3 RESOURCES

- CDC: Violence Prevention - Adverse Childhood Experiences (https://www.cdc.gov/violenceprevention/childabuseandneglect/acestudy/index.html)
- 9 Types of Hopelessness and How to Overcome Them (https://psychcentral.com/blog/the-9-types-of-hopelessness-and-how-to-overcome-them/)
- ACEs Aware (https://www.acesaware.org/)
- Big Brothers, Big Sisters (https://www.bbbs.org/)
- Welcoming Schools (https://www.welcomingschools.org/)
- Selena Gomez Biography (https://www.biography.com/musician/selena-gomez)

ADDITIONAL RESOURCES

- The Clay Center for Young, Healthy Minds (https://www.mghclaycenter.org/)
- Erica's Lighthouse (https://www.erikaslighthouse.org/)
- The Trevor Project (https://www.thetrevorproject.org/)
- Born This Way Foundation (https://bornthisway.foundation/)
- "Screenagers" Documentary (https://www.screenagersmovie.com/)
- "The Mask You Live In" Documentary (http://therepresentationproject.org/film/the-mask-you-live-in-film/)
- Inner Explorer (https://innerexplorer.org/)

ADDITIONAL RESOURCES

Hopeful Minds is based on the research that hope is teachable. The aim is to equip all students, teachers, and parents with the tools they need to define, learn, and grow a Hopeful Mind. The Hopeful Minds curriculums and resources are available for download at www.hopefulminds.org/curriculums

The Five-Day Global Hope Challenge is a daily challenge that introduces the Five Keys to Shine Hope that everyone can use to activate hope within their lives and their community. The challenge is ideal for governments, workplaces, schools, and more. Sign-up today at www.hopefulcities.org

Friendship Bench's mission is to get people out of kufungisisa - depression & anxiety - by creating safe spaces and a sense of belonging in communities to improve mental wellbeing and enhance quality of life. To learn more and request a bench placed in your area, visit
www.friendshipbenchzimbabwe.org

Karma Box Project is a community initiative allowing people to give non-perishable food, hygiene products, toiletries, and other useful items to those in need. The boxes are filled up with the goods by anyone in the community and someone in need can take items from the box as needed. To learn more, visit www.karmaboxproject.org

One World Strong Foundation created the ResilienceNet Mobile App, which empowers and provides support to local, regional, and national terrorism prevention practitioners, relevant frontline responders and individual Americans seeking support. To learn more about the One World Strong Foundation and download their app, visit www.oneworldstrong.org/copy-of-how-we-do-it

National Alliance on Mental Illness (NAMI) is America's largest grassroots mental health organization dedicated to building better lives for Americans affected by mental illness. NAMI offers an abundance of resources for those navigating mental illness or for those seeking to learn more.
Find more at www.nami.org/home

Choose Love Movement nurtures safer and more loving communities through next generation essential life skills and character development programs for all stages of life. Choose Love is an evidence-based curriculum that will help students feel safer, learn better, and achieve more! Find out more at www.chooselovemovement.org

Hope Means Nevada works to eliminate teen suicide and empower Nevada's youth to live hopeful lives. Find out more at www.hopemeansnevada.org

One Mind catalyzes visionary change through science, business and media to transform the world's mental health. Find out more at www.onemind.org

Charter for Compassion supports the emerging global movement that brings compassion to life. It is a global network connecting people, cities, grassroots organizers and leaders to each other. It provides educational resources, organizing tools, and avenues for communication. Find out more at
www.charterforcompassion.org

Hopeful Mindsets®

Hopeful Mindsets® is a framework that uses the Five Keys to Shine Hope to apply to any challenge in life. It is based on the work of leading experts on Hope, Mindset, Mental Health, Stress, Positive Psychology, Business, Communications, and more. Using the Five Keys to Shine Hope as a foundation, Hopeful Mindsets introduces critical hope skills to help anyone move from hopelessness to hope.

The initial program, Hopeful Mindsets on the College Campus, is a 10-module video course from The Shine Hope Company that equips students with crucial hope skills through expert insights and real-life stories. The course features experts from Harvard, Stanford, and Columbia, with insights from recent college graduates that offer real-life practical strategies and stories from their experiences with homelessness, mental health diagnoses, death, violence, and everyday challenges at school.

The Hopeful Mindsets General Overview is a 90-minute video course for anyone that introduces hope and the Five Keys to Shine Hope framework to help you create, maintain, and grow hope in your life. This course is taught by Kathryn Goetzke, based on her knowledge of mental health and hope, and her work to date. It compiles knowledge from leading experts on Hope, Mindset, Mental Health, Stress, Positive Psychology, Business, Communications, and includes video lessons, a full downloadable workbook and exercises to practice skills for hope, and is available individually or to license for organizations.

The Hopeful Mindsets Workplace Overview is a 90-minute video course for the workplace that introduces hope and the Five Keys to Shine Hope™ framework to help you create, maintain, and grow hope in the workplace. We give an overview of the framework, so you can then apply it to your career to activate hope at work. The course is available for individuals or to license to entire companies, to ensure all know the what, why, and how of hope.

You can learn more about the Hopeful Mindsets courses at www.hopecourses.com.

HOPEFUL MINDS OVERVIEW: Additional Resources for Educators

Hopeful Cities

Hopeful Cities© is equipping cities around the world with the tools they need to create, maintain, and grow hope, citywide. Learn how you can activate hope in your community at www.hopefulcities.org.

Hopeful Minds

Hopeful Minds® is programming for youth based on research that suggests hope is teachable (a skill). The aim is to equip students, teachers, and parents with the tools they need to define, learn, and grow Hopeful Minds in young kids. Learn more at www.hopefulminds.org.

the shine hope company

The Shine Hope Company™ - Our mission is to improve lives globally by teaching scientifically informed and evidence-based methods to measure and cultivate hope. Learn how to activate hope in your life and community at www.theshinehopecompany.com.

Resources for Stress, Anxiety, and Depression

CHILDREN AND STRESS

Stress is the product of the demands that are placed on us, and a normal part of life. It is not stress that kills us, it is our inability to effectively manage stress. Friends, family, jobs, or school can create stress, as well as a disconnection between what we think we should be accomplishing and what we are actually able to accomplish.

Children are not immune to stress, and if your child is feeling stress they are not alone. Some research suggests children are even more stressed than adults in these times. There are many reasons your children may encounter stress. Our Hopeful Minds program addresses stress, and provides stress management techniques, including the key 90 second rule. Our goal is to share additional insights, and provide tips on what else you might do at home.

As children grow, academic and social pressures, world news, and external trauma can become stressors at an increasing rate. The symptoms of stress can vary; however, the following list contains some of the more common symptoms typically identified in children suffering from stress:

- Stomachaches,
- Headaches and Nightmares
- Trouble concentrating or completing schoolwork
- Overreacting to minor problems
- Becoming clingy
- Becoming withdrawn or spending more time alone
- Short-term behavioral changes, such as mood swings, acting out, bedwetting, and changes in sleep pattern
- Younger children may start thumb sucking, hair twirling, and nose picking
- Older children may begin lying, bullying, or defying authority
- Drastic changes in academic performance

SOLUTIONS TO STRESS

There are healthy ways to help children both cope with and minimize stressors in their lives. We've provided a number of solutions in our Hopeful Minds program, and encourage you to do it with them so they start to recognize "stress," know how it feels in their body, and proactively manage it. It isn't stress that hurts us, it is our inability to manage stress. In addition to practicing hope strategies with them, you can support your child in managing their stress in the following ways:

AT HOME

- Download our Parent's Guide at www.hopefulminds.org/curriculums, and start using hope language at home.
- Make sure your child is getting proper rest and nutrition. Children need a well-balanced diet and 9-12 hours of sleep each night to stay physically and mentally healthy.
- Ensure your home is a physically and emotionally safe place for your child to come home to.
- Commit to a routine.
- Monitor the amount of screen time, as well as the television, video game, and book content your child is ingesting. The following two articles give excellent insights into the problems that can arise from too much screen time during childhood.
    - https://gabb.com/blog/how-smart-phones-affect-brain-development/
    - https://gabb.com/blog/austin-weirichs-story/
- Don't overschedule. Too many extracurricular activities can increase stress.
- Take time to talk through changes with your child before they happen.
- Encourage children to perform visualization and breathing activities prior to stressful events, such as games and tests.
- Learn to listen to problems without being critical or solving the problems for them. Help your children find their own solutions to situations that are adding stress to their lives.
- At the start of conversations with your children, establish whether they want you to listen, give advice, or take action based on the information they are sharing.
- Provide affection and encouragement.
- Adopt healthy habits, such as exercise and self-care, to manage your own stress in healthy ways. Children are perceptive and will pick up on how you react to your own stressors.

AT SCHOOL

- Involve students in social, club, and athletic activities where they can succeed.
- Use positive reinforcement and methods of discipline that promote self-esteem.
- Limit homework overload.
- Take time to actively listen to students and help them find ways to decrease stressors in their lives.
- Use frequent "movement" breaks between lessons to keep students active and engaged.
- Schedule time to organize. Especially in lower grades, providing time to organize desks and cubbies, sharpen pencils, and put away toys and tools can give students a greater sense of control.
- Establish a routine and implement your own time management techniques. A hectic classroom schedule is a common stressor for students.
- Encourage students to perform visualization and breathing activities prior to stressful events, such as games and tests.
- Pay attention to behavioral changes in your students. If concerning behaviors are continually exhibited, reach out to parents and/or a counselor.
- Provide patience and encouragement.

CHILDREN AND ANXIETY

When stress is not properly mitigated, it can lead to anxiety. Anxiety disorders negatively impact a child's life in many ways. Most children have fears and worries that appear at different times during development. Although fears and worries are normal, persistent or extreme fears may be due to anxiety.

The general rule is if any of these symptoms appear for two or more weeks, and are disrupting your child's daily life and activities, it is best to seek advice from a medical professional. The following is a list of symptoms that may help you determine if your child is experiencing anxiety:

- Distress during separation
- Phobias
- Fear and discomfort in social settings
- Excessive worry about the future and bad things happening
- Abnormal irritation or anger
- Trouble sleeping and fatigue
- Headaches and Stomachaches
- Repeated episodes of sudden, unexpected fear that come with symptoms such as heart pounding, trouble breathing, feeling dizzy, shaking, and sweating

MANAGING ANXIETY

As a parent or teacher, your goal isn't to eliminate a child's anxiety, but to help them learn to manage it. If you believe your child may have anxiety, it is important to take active steps to get your child the help they need including talking to a medical professional like your primary care doctor, or a therapist.

There is no shame in seeking support. Just as you would encourage your child to get support for heart or lung issues, kids need to feel comfortable seeking help for their brain. Mental health is a unique interplay of behavioral and biological exchange, so it is important to work on both. You can help them manage their anxiety in the following ways:

AT HOME

- Consult with your child's pediatrician or family physician. A mental health assessment and evaluation can be done for a diagnosis and treatment plan. Your doctor may refer you to a mental health professional such as a psychiatrist, psychologist, or counselor. *(Do not delay treatment. Early detection and diagnosis are important for getting your child the help they need. Though parents or guardians can often feel responsible for what is happening with their children, they did not cause the anxiety.)*
- Respect your child's feelings but don't empower the feelings. It is important to acknowledge that their feelings are real and valid and help them find the source of the anxiety they are feeling. However, once they have acknowledged their anxiety, it is important to help children learn to face their fears. Make sure you are not reinforcing fears with your behaviors.
- Make sure your child is getting proper rest and nutrition. Children need a well-balanced diet and 9-12 hours of sleep each night to stay physically and mentally healthy.
- Ensure your home is a physically and emotionally safe place for your child to come home to.
- Commit to a routine.
- Monitor the amount of screen time, as well as the television, video game, and book content your child is ingesting.
- Practice mindfulness and relaxation techniques.
- Take time to talk through changes with your child before they happen. Preparing for upcoming changes can help remove the anxiety associated with them.
- At the start of conversations with your children, establish whether they want you to listen, give advice, or take action based on the information they are sharing.
- Help your child with problem-solving skills. Develop a plan of realistic steps your child can take toward a goal, recognize their success on the path, and encourage the enjoyment of the experience along the way. Help identify potential obstacles or difficulties and plan/talk about ways to overcome them. Focus on strengths.
- Adopt healthy habits to manage your own anxieties. Children are perceptive and will pick up on how you react to your own anxieties.
- Have conversations with your children about failure. It is important for them to understand that everyone fails at things and that when they fail, it does not mean that they are failures.

AT SCHOOL

- Use positive reinforcement and methods of discipline that promote self-esteem.
- Respect your student's feelings but don't empower the feelings. It is important to acknowledge that their feelings are valid and help them find the source of the anxiety they are feeling. However, once they have acknowledged their anxiety, it is important to help children learn to face their fears. Make sure you are not reinforcing fears with your behaviors.
- Limit homework overload.
- Take time to actively listen to students and help them find ways to decrease stressors in their lives.
- Schedule time to organize. Especially in lower grades, providing time to organize desks and cubbies, sharpen pencils, and put away toys and tools can give students a greater sense of control.
- Encourage students to face their anxieties in baby steps. Come up with techniques that allow them to participate a bit more each time.
- Establish a routine and implement your own time management techniques. A hectic classroom schedule is a common stressor for students.
- Encourage students to perform visualization and breathing activities prior to stressful events, such as games and tests.
- Pay attention to student interactions to prevent bullying and abuse within your classroom.
- Pay attention to behavioral changes in your students. If concerning behaviors are continually exhibited, check your school's policy and reach out to parents, guardians and/or a counselor.
- Provide patience and encouragement.
- Have conversations with your students about failure. It is important for them to understand that everyone fails at things and that when they fail, it does not mean that they are failures.

CHILDREN AND DEPRESSION

Depression is a serious mood disorder that can take the joy from a child's life. It is normal for a child to be moody or sad from time to time. However, if these feelings last more than two weeks, and start to interfere with daily activities, it may be a sign of clinical depression. The following list of symptoms may help you identify if a child is experiencing depression.

- Frequent sadness, or crying more often or more easily
- Poor concentration
- Increased irritability, anger, or hostility
- Hopelessness
- Decreased interest in activities, or an inability to enjoy usual activities
- Persistent boredom or low energy
- Social isolation/withdrawal: Spending more time alone, away from family and friends
- Violence towards self or others
- "Clingy" and more dependent behavior in certain relationships
- Overly pessimistic attitude or excessive guilt
- Feelings of worthlessness and extreme sensitivity to rejection or failure
- Difficulty with relationships
- Over or under eating, or any form of addictive behavior
- Frequent complaints of physical illnesses, such as headaches and stomachaches
- Frequent absences from school or poor performance in school
- Major changes in eating and/or sleeping patterns
- Talk of, or efforts to, run away from home
- Self-destructive behavior or self-harm
- Thoughts of death or expressions of suicide
- Increase in risk-taking behaviors and/or showing less concern for their own safety
- Younger children may act younger than their age (regression)
- Low self-esteem

MANAGING DEPRESSION

Depression may look different in a child than in an adult, and therefore many children do not get the treatment they need. If you believe your child may be depressed, it is important to take active steps to get your child the help they need. You can help them manage their depression in the following ways:

AT HOME

- Consult with your child's pediatrician or family physician. A mental health assessment and evaluation can be done for a diagnosis and treatment plan. Your doctor may refer you to a mental health professional such as a psychiatrist, psychologist, or counselor. *(Do not delay treatment. Early detection and diagnosis are important for getting your child the help they need. Though parents can often feel responsible for what is happening with their children, they did not cause the depression.)*
- Respect your child's feelings but don't empower the feelings. It is important to acknowledge that their feelings are real and valid and help them find the source of the anxiety they are feeling. However, once they have acknowledged their anxiety, it is important to help children learn to face their fears. Make sure you are not reinforcing fears with your behaviors.
- Make sure your child is getting proper rest and nutrition. Children need a well-balanced diet and 9-12 hours of sleep each night to stay physically and mentally healthy.
- Life stressors such as an illness, a separation/divorce, a move, or death can trigger short-term problems or lead to depression. Under these stressors, it is helpful for families to turn to a mental health professional. Depression is treatable, but, if left untreated, can be life threatening. Depression is a major risk factor for suicide.
- Communicate with your child's school. Teachers, school psychologists, and social workers are there to help.
- Talk to your child and listen carefully. Never dismiss feelings, but point out realities and offer hope.
- Remind your child that you are always there to help and support them. Depressed children need continual reassurance. It is common for them to feel unworthy when experiencing depression.
- Remind your child that they are important and needed.
- Encourage and be a positive role model for a healthy lifestyle. Getting proper nutrition, having adequate sleep, and exercising all help alleviate stress, build relationships, and improve mood.

- Help your child with problem-solving skills. Develop a plan of realistic steps your child can take toward a goal, recognize their success on the path, and encourage the enjoyment of the experience along the way. Help identify potential obstacles or difficulties and plan/talk about ways to overcome them. Focus on strengths.
- Never ignore statements and comments about death or suicide. Report them to your child's doctor immediately and if you believe your child is in immediate danger do not leave them alone. Contact your local emergency room in the US; or numbers at the end of this document. You may develop a safety and emergency plan of your own. Have a list of numbers ready to call.

AT SCHOOL

- Communicate with the student's parents, as well as the school psychologists and social workers.
- Talk to your student and listen carefully. Never dismiss feelings, but point out realities and offer hope.
- Use positive reinforcement and methods of discipline that promote self-esteem.
- Use frequent "movement" breaks between lessons to keep students active and engaged. Exercise can help decrease depression and increase mindfulness.
- Schedule time to organize. Especially in lower grades, providing time to organize desks and cubbies, sharpen pencils, and put away toys and tools can give students a greater sense of control.
- Establish a routine and implement your own time management techniques. A hectic classroom schedule can be an additional stressful obstacle for students to deal with.
- Remind your student that you are always there to help and support them. Depressed children need continual reassurance. It is common for them to feel unworthy when experiencing depression.
- Help your student with problem-solving skills. Develop a plan of realistic steps your student can take toward an academic goal, recognize their success on the path, and encourage the enjoyment of the experience along the way. Help identify potential obstacles or difficulties and plan/talk about ways to overcome them. Focus on strengths.
- Never ignore statements and comments about death or suicide. Report them to the school counselor and the student's parents immediately. If you believe your student is in immediate danger do not leave them alone. Contact your local emergency room in the US; or numbers at the end of this document. You may develop a safety and emergency plan of your own. Have a list of numbers ready to call.

RESEARCH CITED

The information provided in this document was obtained from the following sources:

1. Childhood Stress. Kidshealth.org (updated February 2015).
2. Stress in School. Community for Accredited Online Schools (updated 2019).
3. Anxiety and Depression in Children, CDC Children's Mental Health (updated March 30, 2020).
4. What to Do (and Not Do) When Children are Anxious, Child Mind Institute.
5. How to Help a Child Struggling with Anxiety. NPR (published October 29, 2019).
6. Depression in Children and Teens. Web MD (updated May 2013).
7. Medical Reference from Healthwise, Incorporated.
8. Adolescent Depression: What Parents Can Do To Help.
9. HealthyChildren.org (updated February 2018).

Where to Find Support

U.S. SUICIDE HOTLINES AND IMMEDIATE TELEPHONE SUPPORT

If you or someone you know needs immediate help in the U.S., call any of the lines for hope below to talk to someone in your local area. They can listen to you and direct you to local resources if further assistance is needed. If someone has talked to you about suicide, and you believe they are currently a threat to themselves or someone else but won't take your help, call 911.

988	**United States Crisis Hotline.** *Hours: Available 24 hours. Languages: English, Spanish.*
(888)628-9454	**National Suicide Prevention Lifeline:** *Spanish Language Available*
(800)799-4889	**National Suicide Prevention Lifeline:** *Deaf & Hard of Hearing Options*
(800)784-2432	**1-800-SUICIDA Spanish Speaking Suicide Hotline**
(877)968-8454	**1-877-YOUTHLINE Teen to Teen Peer Counseling Hotline**
(866)488-7386	**TrevorLifeLine for LGBTQ Support**
(877)565-8860	**Trans Lifeline**

You can also text HOME to 741741 to connect with a crisis counselor from *crisistextline.org.*

If you are in need of support, you can find additional resources by visiting www.ifred.org/individual-support or scanning the QR Code.

TO FIND A LIST OF INTERNATIONAL RESOURCES VISIT:
www.ifred.org/resources

CDC NATIONAL HEALTH EDUCATION STANDARDS

The National Health Education Standards (NHES) were developed to establish, promote, and support health-enhancing behaviors for students in all grade levels—from pre-Kindergarten through grade 12. The NHES provides a framework for teachers, administrators, and policy makers in designing or selecting curricula, allocating instructional resources, and assessing student achievement and progress. Importantly, the standards provide students, families and communities with concrete expectations for health education.

ILLINOIS STATE STANDARDS FOR SOCIAL/EMOTIONAL LEARNING CURRICULUM ALIGNMENT

The state of Illinois defines social and emotional learning as "the process through which children and adults acquire knowledge, attitudes, and skills they need to:"

- Recognize and manage their emotions
- Demonstrate caring and concern for others
- Establish positive relationships
- Make responsible decisions
- Handle challenging situations constructively

Further, "Quality SEL instruction in which students learn to process, integrate, and selectively apply SEL skills in developmentally, contextually, and culturally appropriate ways in conjunction with a safe, caring, participatory and responsive school climate can result in positive outcomes including:"

- Promotion of mental wellness
- Prevention of mental health issues
- School connectedness
- Reduction in student absenteeism
- Reduction in suspensions
- Adoption, implementation, and institutionalization of new practices
- Improved academic outcomes

You can check www.hopefulminds.org/curriculums and download our guide that reviews how for each lesson for the Overview and Deep Dive programs meet these CDC guidelines.

www.ingramcontent.com/pod-product-compliance
Lightning Source LLC
Chambersburg PA
CBHW080412120526
44589CB00037BB/2679